T5-BSH-905

THE

SACRED BOOKS

OF THE

HINDUS.

TRANSLATED BY

VARIOUS SANSKRIT SCHOLARS

EDITED BY

Major B. D. Basu, I. M. S. (Retired).

VOLUME XXX.—Part 2.

THE TAITIRIYA UPANISAT.

TRANSLATED BY

Rai Bahadur Srisa Chandra Vidyarnava

and

Pandit Mohan Lal Sandal, M. A., L. L. B.

PUBLISHED BY

Major B. D. Basu, I. M. S. (Retired), at the Panini Office,

Bhuvaneswari Asram, Bahadurganj, Allahabad.

Printed by R. S. Gupta at the Agarwal Printing Works, Allahabad.

Library of Congress Cataloging in Publication Data

Upanishads. Taittiriyopanisad. English and Sanskrit.
The Tait[t]iriya Upanisat.

Original ed. issued as v. 30, pt. 3 of The Sacred books of the Hindus.
English and Sanskrit; commentary in English.
I. Vasu, Srisa Chandra, rai bahadur, 1861-1918?, ed.
II. Sandal, Mohan Lal, ed. III. Title. IV. Series: The Sacred books of the Hindus, v. 30, pt. 3.
BL1120.A732 1974 294.5'921 73-3824
ISBN 0-404-57833-0

Reprinted from the edition of 1925, Allahabad
First AMS edition published, 1974
Manufactured in the United States of America

International Standard Book Number:
Complete Set: 0-404-57800-4
Volume 30, pt. 2: 0-404-57833-0

AMS Press, INC.
New York, N.Y. 10003

THE
AITAREYA UPANIṢAT.

TRANSLATED BY

Rai Bahadur Srisa Chandra Vidyarnava

and

Pandit Mohan Lal Sandal, M. A., L. L. B.

PUBLISHED BY

Major B. D. Basu, I. M. S. (Retired), at the Panini Office,

Bhuvaneswari Asram, Bahadurganj, Allahabad.

[1925]

Taittirîya Upanisat.

I. Sıkṣa-vallî.

Peace Chant.

ॐ ओंशन्नोमित्रः शंवरुणः। शन्नोभवत्वर्यमा। शन्नइंद्रो-
बृहस्पतिः। शन्नोविष्णुरुरुक्रमः। नमो ब्रह्मणे। नमस्ते-
वायो। त्वमेवप्रत्यक्षंब्रह्मासि। त्वामेवप्रत्यक्षंब्रह्मवदिष्यामि।
ऋतंवदिष्यामिसत्यंवदिष्यामि। तन्मामवतु। तद्वक्तारमवतु।
अवतुमां। अवतुवक्तारं। ओंशांतिः शांतिः शांतिः ॥१॥

ओं om, a mystic syllable; शं śaṃ, favourable; नः naḥ, to us; मित्रः god Mitra; शं śaṃ, favourable; वरुणः varuṇaḥ, god Varuṇa; शं śaṃ, favourable; नः naḥ, to us; भवतु bhavatu, be अर्यमा Aryamà, the god of that name; शं śaṃ, favourable; नः naḥ, to us; इंद्रः Indraḥ, the god of that name; बृहस्पति Brihaspati, the god of that name; शं śaṃ, favourable; नः naḥ, to us; विष्णुः Viṣṇu, the god of that name; उरुक्रमः urukramaḥ, of powerful strîde; नमः namaḥ, salutation; ब्रह्मणे brahmaṇe, to Brahma; नमः namaḥ, salutation; ते Te, to thee; वायो Vâyo, to Vâyu; त्वम् Tvam, thou; एव Eva, indeed; alone; प्रत्यक्षम् pratyakṣam, visible, literally in front of every eye or residing in and controlling the senses; ब्रह्म Brahma, असि Asi, art; त्वाम् tvâm, thee एव eva, even; प्रत्यक्षम् pratyakṣam, visible as existing in animate bodies, as prâṇa, apâna etc., ब्रह्म Brahma, Brahman, वदिष्यामि vadiṣyâmi, I shall call or declare; ऋतम् ṛitam, lord of righteousness; वदिष्यामि vadiṣyâmi, I shall declare; सत्यम् satyam, with true knowledge; truly, speaker and doer of what is right; तत् tat, therefore; माम् mâm, me, अवतु avatu, may thou protect, तत् tat, therefore, वक्तारम् vaktâram, the speaker; अवतु avatu, protect thou; अवतु avatu, protect thou; माम्

mâm, me ; अवतु avatu, protect thou ; वक्तारम् vaktâram, the speaker ; ओम् Om, शान्तिः sântiḥ, (thrice), peace, peace, and peace.

1. Om ! Let Mitra be favourable to us, let Varuṇa be favourable to us, let Indra and Brihaspati be favourable to us, let Viṣṇu of powerful strides be favourable to us. Salutation be to Brahma, let salutation be to thee, O Vâyu. Thou art alone visible Brahma, I shall speak of thee as visible Brahma. I shall speak right, I shall speak truth. Therefore protect me, protect its speaker. Protect me, protect the speaker. Om, be peace, peace, peace.

Commentary.

The ṛiṣis of the upniṣad are Viṣṇu who pervades the Sun, Brahmâ, Varuṇa and Bhrigu. Hari is the deity. There is no need for enquiry as to the metre. It may be considered Anuṣṭup. Bhrigu in order to study the spiritual science (Brahma Vidyâ) prays to gods to remove the obstacles. Let Mitra confer happiness on him and so on. Vâyu being principal in the study of spiritual science and the chief god of Brahma, is separately saluted. He is called Brahma being a principal deity appointed by Brahma; there is a Vedic verse 'प्राणोब्रह्म' 'vital air' is Brahma. Having saluted Vâyu in the spiritual form, he salutes him in his divine or elemental form. He is called visible, because speech is called Brahma by the Kâṇva school "वाग्वै ब्रह्म" Vâyu pervades the human body in five forms called Prâṇa, Apâna, Udâna, Vyâna and Samâna, As to their full description, see at p. p. 15 and 16 of the Siddhânta Darśanam, Volume XXVIII of the S. B. H. He prays for the protection of both the teacher and the pupil. The word 'peace' is thrice repeated in order to ward off the terrestial, aerial and heavenly calamities.

शीक्षांव्याख्यास्यामः । वर्णःस्वरः । मात्राबलं । सामसंतानः । इत्युक्तःशीक्षाध्यायः ॥ २ ॥

ओम् Om ; शीक्षाम् śikṣâm, which is to be learnt ; व्याख्यास्यामः vyâkhyâsyâmaḥ, we shall explain ; वर्णः varṇaḥ, letter; the place where the particular sound is originated, adorable; स्वरः swaraḥ, accent, self-sporting, self-enjoying; मात्रा mâtrâ, the quality, the accent ; बलम् balam. the efforts in the utterance of letters साम sâma, modulation, conjoining of the same letters in all forms; सन्तानः santânaḥ, series of letters, possessing a string of auspicious qualities. The union of letters or sandhi : इति iti, thus; उक्तः uktaḥ, called; शीक्षाध्यायः the lecture on siksa.

2. We shall explain orthoepy ; the letters are accents, the syllables are power; the songs are alphabets. Thus the chapter on orthoepy is explained.

Commentary.

Orthoepy is a science of pronounciation, because, it is highly necessary before learning the spiritual science. Here in the text, 'letter' means guttural, palatial, cerebral, dental and labial; the accent means high, low and middle tunes; syllable means one or two, syllables etc.; power means endeavour to pronounce letters. The letters of a song constitute alphabets. 'Letter' represents Viṣṇu So much is the chapter on orthoepy.

सहनौयशः । सहनौब्रह्मवर्चसं । अथात·सँहितायाउपनिषदं व्याख्यास्यामः । पंचस्वधिकरणेषु । अधिलोकमधिज्यौतिष- मधिविद्यमधिप्रजमध्यात्मं । तामहासँहिताइत्याचक्षते ॥ ३ ॥

सह saha, to, नौ nau, to us both, the teacher and student; यशः yaśaḥ, Glory ; ब्रह्मवर्चसम् brahmavarchasam, the Vedic light ; अथ atha, now : अतः ataḥ, hence, संहितायाः saṅhitâyâḥ, of the collection of the Vedic mantras ; उपनिषदम् upaniṣadam, the secret ; पञ्चसु pañchasu, in five; अधिकरणेषु adhikaraṇeṣu, heads ; अधिलोकम् adhilokam, with regard to the worlds ; अधिज्यौतिषम् adhijyautiṣam, with regard to heavenly lights ; अधिविद्यम्, adhividyam, with regards to knowledge ; अधिप्रजम् adhiprajam, with regards to offspring ; अध्यात्मम्, adhyâtmam with regards to the self ; ताः tâḥ, the above, these ; महासंहिताः mahâ saṃhitâḥ, great samhita ; इति iti, by this name, thus ; आचक्षते achakṣate, they call.

3. Let fame come to us both ; let Brahmaṇic glory come to us both. Now we shall explain the mystery of the combination (samhita) into five parts, with regard to worldly region, light, knowledge, progeny and soul. They call it great combination (samhita).

Commentary

Having invoked the deities in the preceding verses the preceptor and the disciple are made to recite the verse with a view to remove the obstacles in their Vedic study. "Let the deities mentioned above be propitious to us, so that we may both obtain fame and glory." Now the verse proceeds to explain the mystery of the combination consisting of the first letter, the subsequent letter, union and means of union. The subject is divided into five heads; they pertain to worldly region, heavenly lights, knowledge, offspring and human body which is called soul' here. The combination represents the different forms of the Lord such us Nârâyaṇa, Vâsudeva &c.; out of respect it is called the grent combination as elucidating the spiritnal knowledge.

अथाधिलोकं । पृथिवीपूर्वंरूपं । द्यौरुत्तररूपं । आकाशः संधिः । वायुःसंधानं । इत्यधिलोकं ॥४॥

अथ atha, now; **आधिलोकम्** adhilokam; **पृथिवी** prithivi, the earth; **पूर्वरूपम्** pûrva rûpam, first elementary form; **द्यौः** : dyauḥ, heaven; **उत्तररूपम्** uttara rûpam, the latter elementary from **आकाशः** âkâśaḥ, ether **संधिः** sandhiḥ, union; **वायुः** vâyuḥ, air; **संधानम्** saṃdhânam, the means of effecting the union; **इति** iti, showing the way in which adhilokam is explained

4. Now as to the wordly region; the earth is the first letter; the heaven is the second letter; ether is their union; air is the means of union. So far pertains to the worldly region.

Commentary.

The verse explains the four forms of the Lord pervading the regions. Vâsudeva, the form of Nârâyaṇa pervades the earth and represents the first letter; Samkarṣaṇa, another manifested form pervades heaven and represents the second letter. Pradyumna who pervades ether is the result of the union, while Aniruddha is the means of this union. Thus we have four forms of the Lord in the worldly region.

अथाधिज्यौतिषं ॥ अग्निः पूर्वंरूपं ॥ आदित्यउत्तररूपं ॥ आपः संधि ॥ वैद्युतः संधानं ॥ इत्यधिज्यौतिषं ॥५॥

अथ atha, now; **अधिज्यौतिषं** adhijyotiṣaṃ, as regards heavenly light; **अग्निः** agniḥ, fire; **पूर्वरूपं**, pûrvarûpam, the preceding form, the first letter; **आदित्यः** adityaḥ, the sun; **उत्तररूपं** uttararûpam, succeeding form or letter; **आपः** âpaḥ, waters; **संधि** saṃdhi, union; **वैद्युतः** vaidyutaḥ, lightning; **संधानं**, saṃdhânaṃ, means of union; **इति**, iti, so far; **अधिज्यौतिषं** adhijyotiṣam, relating to heavenly light.

5. Now as regards heavenly light ; fire is the first letter ; the sun is the second letter ; water is union, lightning is the means of union. So far relates to heavenly light.

Commentary.

Now the verse after the description of the worldly regions given in the preceding verse explains the mystery of heavenly lights. The elemental fire pervaded by Vâsudeva represents the first letter ; the sun pervaded by Saṃkarṣaṇa represents the second letter. Pradyumna pervading the waters is the result of the union ; Aniruddha pervading the lightning is the means of the union. So much we have about heavenly lights.

अथाधिविद्यं । आचार्यःपूर्वरूपं । अन्तेवास्युत्तररूपं । विद्या-संधिः । प्रवचनँसंधानं । इत्यधिविद्यं ॥ ६ ॥

अथ atha, now; **अधिविद्यम्**, adhividyam ; **आचार्यः** âcharyaḥ, **आचार्यस्थं आचार्य नामकं संकर्षणं वासुदेवात्मकं, रूपम्** । the godly form residing in a teacher ; **पूर्व-रूपम्**, pûrvarûpam, **पूर्ववर्ण प्रतिपाद्यम्**, denoting the first syllable, first born ; **अन्तेवासी**, antevâsî, **अन्तेवासिस्थं अन्ते वासिनामकं संकर्षणं संकर्षणात्मकं रूपं** । that form of god in a disciple ; **उत्तररूपम्**, uttararûpam ; **विद्या**, vidyâ, **गुरुशिष्यसंघर्षजं ज्ञानं** । learning (that which comes out of the mutual labour of the teacher and the taught) ; **प्रवचनम्**, pravachanam, **प्रवचनस्थं प्रवचननामकम् संकर्षणानुरुद्धाख्यंरूपं** । existing in the teachings (especially of the Vedas) ; **सन्धानम्**, saṇdhḥanaṃ, means of union ; **इति अधिविद्यम्**,

6. Now as to knowledge ; the preceptor represents the first letter ; the resident student is the second letter ; knowledge is the union ; the Vedic study is the means of union. So far pertains to knowledge.

Commentary.

The verse is to be explained similarly ; Vâsudeva who is preceptor represents the first letter : Saṃkarṣaṇa who is the resident student represents the second letter. Pradyumna the third form of the Lord represents knowledge which is the combined result of the preceptor and the pupil. Aniruddha representing the Vedic study is the means of union. So much relates to knowledge.

अथाधिप्रजं । मातापूर्वरूपं । पितोत्तररूपं । प्रजासंधिः । प्रजननसंधानं । इत्यधिप्रजं ॥ ७ ॥

अथ, अधिप्रजम्, माता, mâtâ, मातृस्थं मातृनामकं प्रद्युम्नंवासुदेवाख्यं रूपम्, that form of god in a mother; संकर्षणात्मकं रूपम्, samkarsaṇâtmakaṃrūpam, that form of god in father; प्रजा, prajâ, प्रजास्थं प्रजानामकं प्रद्युम्नप्रद्युम्नात्मकं रूपम्। that form of god in progeny; संधिः, प्रजननम्, prajananam, प्रजननस्थं प्रजनननामकं प्रद्युम्नानिरुद्धात्मकम् रूपम। that form of god exhibited by procreation;

7. Now as regards offspring; the mother is the first letter; the father is the second letter; progeny is the union; procreation is the means of union: So far relates to offspring.

Commentary.

The verse is to be explained similarly. Vhsudeva representing mother stands for the first letter; Saṃkarṣaṇa representing the father stands for the second letter. Pradayumna representing the offspring is the result of the union. Procreation which is the means of union is represnted by Aniruddha. It relates to offspring

अथाध्यात्मं अधराहनुः पूर्वरूपं । उत्तराहनुरुत्तररूपं । वाक्संधिः । जिह्वासंधानं । इत्यध्यात्मं । इतीमामहासंहिताः । यएवमेतामहासंहिताव्याख्याता वेद । संधीयते- प्रजयापशुभिः । ब्रह्मवर्चसेनान्नाद्येनसुवर्गेणलोकेन ॥ ८ ॥

अथ atha Now; अध्यात्मं adhytyâtmam, as regards soul. पूर्वरूपम् purva-rupam, the preceding form, the first letter. अधराहनुः, adharâ hanuḥ, तत्स्थं तन्नामकं अनिरुद्धवासुदेवात्मकं रूपम्। the form of god which resides in the lower jaw; (अधरा) (हनुः) उत्तराहनुः, uttarâ hanuḥ, तत्स्थं तन्नामकं अनिरुद्धसंकर्षणात्मकंरूपम्। that form of god existing in the upper (उत्तरा) jaw; वाक्, vâk, वागिन्द्रियस्थं तन्नामकं अनिरुद्धप्रद्युम्नात्मकं रूपम्, that form of god existing in speech; सन्धिः, sandhiḥ; जिह्वा, jivhâ, जिह्वास्थं तन्नामकं अनिरुद्धं अनिरुद्धात्मकं रूपं। that form of god existing in the tongue; सन्धानम्, sandhânam, इति, iti, अध्यात्मम्, adhyâtmam, इति, iti, इमाः, imâḥ, these; महासंहिताः, mahâsaṃhitâh, वेद, veda, उपास्ते, साक्षात्करोति, actually learns: संधीयते, sandhîyate, संयुक्तो भवति, becomes joined to; प्रजया, prajayâ, to progeny, पशुभिः, paśubhiḥ, to cattle; ब्रह्मवर्चसेन, brahmavarchcha-sena, to the Vedic light; अन्नाद्येन, annâdyena, to food and oher such necessaries of life ; सुवर्ग्येण, suvargyeṇa, विष्णुलोकेन, श्वेतद्वीपेन, to the lustrous country vaikunntha ; लोकेन, lokena, to country.

8. Now as regards the soul, the lower jaw is the first form. Speech is the union ; tongue is the means of union : so far relates to soul, This is the great combination. One who understands this great combination, is united with the offspring, cattle, Brahmanic splendour, eatables and heavenly region.

Commentary.

Here the term 'Âtmâ' is used in the sense of body. Vâsudeva representing the lower jaw stands for the first letter. Saṃkarṣaṇa representing the upper jaw stands for the second letter. Pradyumna is speech, the result of the union and Aniruddha, representing the tongue is the means of union. The verse extols this combination, because it relates to Viṣṇu; it is appropriately called the great combination. The fruit that accrues to the devotee who realises the four forms of the Lord, obtains offspring, cattle Brahmanic glory, eatable food and heaven.

यच्छंदसामृषभोविश्वरूपः । छंदोभ्योध्यमृतात्संबभूव । समेंद्रोमेधयास्पृणोतु । अमृतस्यदेवधारणोभूयासं शरीरंमे-विचर्षणं । जिह्वामेमधुमत्तमा । कर्णाभ्यांभूरिविश्रवं ब्रह्मणःकोशोसिमेधयापिहितः श्रुतंमेगोपाय ॥६॥

यः yaḥ, इन्द्रः परमेश्वरः । he who ; छन्दसाम्, chandasâṃ, वेदानाम्, of the Vedas ; ऋषभः, riṣabhaḥ, अधिपति, नियन्ता वा, lord ; विश्वरूपः visvarûpaḥ, पूर्वविग्रहस्वरूप : नानारूपः वा, having all or various forms ; छन्दोभ्यः, chhandobhyaḥ, वेदेभ्यः; out of the Vedas or through the Vedas ; अध्यमृतात्संबभूव, adhyamritât sambabhûva, अमृतात् अधिसंबभूव, (अमृतात्) अमृतेभ्यः नित्येभ्यः (अधि) अधिकतया (संबभूव) सुव्यक्तो ऽभूत्, who was more clearly seen or known through (Vedas) the eternal ; सः, saḥ that ; मा, mâ, me ; इन्द्र, Indraḥ ; मेधया, medhayâ, प्रज्ञया, with Intellectual powers ; स्पृणोतु, spriṇotu, प्रीणयतु बलयतु, may please comfort or strengthen ; अमृतस्य, amritasya, नित्यस्य, वेदानां, of the constant, ever-lasting Vedas ; देव, deva, हे देव, O ! god ! धारणः, dhâraṇaḥ, धारकः, possessor owner and user ; भूयासम्, bhûyâsam; स्याम्, should be ; अमृतस्य धारणो भूयासम्, नित्यस्य वेदस्य धारकः भूयासम्, तत्वज्ञानी भूत्वा क्षिप्रं मुक्तः स्याम् ॥ (O ! god I) should be the possessor of the Vedas (or Vedic philosophy) ; शरीरम्, śarîram, body ; मे, me, मम, my ; विचर्षणम्, vicharṣaṇam, विशिष्टाः चर्षणयः प्रजाः यस्यतत् । विशिष्टशिष्यप्रजायुक्तम् (भूयाम्), endowed with special qualities of a studious boy ; जिह्वा, jivhâ, the tongue; मे, me ; मधुमत्तमा, madhumattamâ, अतिशयेन मधुमती, सुखसाधनभगवद्बोधकवेदोच्चारणवती । exceedingly charming, sweet or effective ; कर्णाभ्याम्, karṇâbhyám with ears भूरि, bhûri, ब्रह्म, much especially about brahma ; विश्रुवम् visruvam, (वि) विशेषेण, (श्रुवम्) ; श्रृणवानि, sriṇavâni, let me hear with extraodinary interest ; ब्रह्मणः, of the Brahma i, e, Veda ; कोशः, kosah, आवासः, treasure-room ; मेधया, medhayâ, with intellectual powers ; पिहित pihitaḥ, अच्छादितः, covered ; श्रुतम्, śrutam, that which is heard (by me) ; मे, me, मया, by me ; गोपाय, gopâya, रक्ष, फलवत्कुरु, protect, help me in retaining, make it useful and fruitful.

9. He is the protector of the Vedas and has many forms ; he is produced from the eternal Vedas. May he, Indra, make me strong with intelligence. O ! God, Let me be a retainer of the eternal (Veda). Let my body be fit ; let my tongue be sweet ; may I hear many things with ears. Thou art the treasure of Brahma covered with intelligence. Protect my learning.

Commentary.

The lord who is invoked in the text is the controller and assumes manifold forms. *Riṣabha* used in the text means 'bull' originally but here it means controller in the secondary sense. There is a Vedic text 'Indra by his tricks assumes many forms'; here he is, therefore, said to assume many forms. The god Indra is here said to be produced from the eternal Vedas. The pupil prays to him to confer strength to his intellect or wisdom, to make him retain the eternal Vedas in his memory, to make his, body fit to produce children and students well versed in learning, to make his tongue sweet or to make him a good orator and to make him hear many branches of learning. The religious student addresses Indra as the treasure house of the Vedic learning and asks him to protect his learning.

आवहंतीवितन्वाना कुर्वाणाचीरमात्मनः । वासाँसिमम गावश्च । अन्नपानेचसर्वदाततोमेश्रियमावह । लोमशां पशुभिः सहस्वाहा ॥१०॥

आवहन्ती âvahantî, आनयन्ती, that which brings, yields ; वितन्वाना, vitanvânâ सनातनी, विस्तारवती, extending over all the periods of time; कुर्वाणा kurvâṇâ, that which manages or arranges ; चीरम्, chîram, चिर सर्वभोगान्, all things of enjoyment and necessaries for all time ; आत्मनः, átmanaḥ, जीवजातस्य, of all the beings ; वासांसि, vâsâṃsi, clothing ; मम, mama, my ; गावः, gâvaḥ, cows, cattle ; च, cha, and; अन्नपाने, annapâne, as eatables and drinkables ; च, cha ; सर्वदा, sarvadâ, always ; ततः, tataḥ, therefore ; मे, me, श्रियम्, śriyaṃ, wealth ; आवह, âvaha, आनय, ; लोमशाम्, lomaśâm, केशवतीम्, a woman full of hair; पशुभिः सह, paśubhiḥ saha, together with the cattle and beasts ; स्वाहा swáhá सुष्ठु आहूयते प्रतिपाद्यते = स्वाहेत्युक्तः गोविन्दः ।

10. Carrying, spreading, making for one's self permanently clothes, cows, food and drink for ever, bring therefore, fortune for me with wooly animals and heads of cattle. Hail.

Commentary.

Carrying in the text means bringing objects of enjoyment for *one's self i.e.*, for the entire created beings or bestowing on the worshipper clothes, cows, food and drink. The religious student prays for such wealth as described above with the heads of cattle. The wooly animal ' in the text means the sheep, goat, etc., who have wool on their body. 'Hail' is a mark of invocation to a deity.

आमायंतुब्रह्मचारिणःस्वाहा । विमायंतुब्रह्मचारिणःस्वाहा । प्रमायंतुब्रह्मचारिणःस्वाहा । दमायंतुब्रह्मचारिणःस्वाहा । शमायंतुब्रह्मचारिणःस्वाहा । यशोजनेसानिस्वाहा । श्रेयान्-वस्यसोसानिस्वाहा । तंत्वाभगप्रविशानिस्वाहा । समाभग-प्रविशस्वाहा । तस्मिन्त्सहस्रशाखे । निभगाहंत्वयिमृजे-स्वाहा ॥११॥

आमायंतु, âmâyantu, मा आयन्तु, मां आयन्तु May come to me; ब्रह्मचारिणः Brahma chârinaḥ, students of the Scriptures; स्वाहा, Svâhâ, विमायन्तु, Vimâyantu मा वि (आ) यन्तु, मां प्रति (वि) विविधाः आयान्तु Let them come from different places and various races; ब्रह्मचारिणः Brahmachâriṇaḥ; स्वाहा Svâhâ; प्रमायन्तु

मा प्र (आ) यन्तु, प्र प्रहृष्टा माम् आयान्तु Let them run forth; (प्र) to me; दमायन्तु, Damâyantu, (दमाः) इन्द्रियनिग्रहवन्तः (आ) यन्तुः आयान्तु, Let them control their senses; शमायन्तु, śamâhyantu शमाः विष्णुनिष्ठावन्त आयान्तु, Let them be devotees of God and enjoy peace; यशः Yaśaḥ fame, publicity, glory; जने jane, amongst the people; असानि, Asâni, भवानि, May become; जने यशः असानि, jane yaśaḥ asâni, जने कीर्तिमान् भवानि, May I be famous as a teacher; श्रेयान्, śreyân, best, greatest; प्रशस्ततरः; वस्यसः, vasyasaḥ, in matters of happiness सुखविषये। असानि, âsâni, स्वाहा, svâhâ, वस्यसः श्रेयान् असानि अविरतसुखवान्स्याम, should be ever happy and comfortable; तम्, tam, him; त्वा tvâ, thee; त्वाम्, tvam, thee; भग, bhaga, O ! treasure possessing all; प्रविशानि, praviśáni, let me enter; सः, sah, he (thou); मा, mâ, भग, bhaga ; प्रविश, praviśa, enter तस्मिन्, tasmin, in that (treasure), त्वयि हे भग, सहस्र शाखे, sahasra şâkhe, in him who is branched in thousands of ways; निभजाहं त्वयिमृजे, nibhajâ ham tvayi mrije,=(हे) भग अहं त्वयि निमृजे पापम्, O ! treasure, I wash myself in thee of my evils; स्वाहा swâhâ, hail.

11. May the religious students come to me, Hail! May various religious students come to me, Hail! May excellent religious students come to me, Hail! May the religious students who have controlled their senses come, Hail! Let peaceful religious students come, Hail! May I be glorious amongst people, Hail! May I be noble and happy, Hail! May I, O! Lord enter thee who art that, Hail! May the Lord enter me, Hail! In thee who hast thousand branches, May I wash (sins) Hail!

Commentary.

In the present verse, the spiritual preceptor prays for the purpose of teaching which is not possible without the religious students. The reader will mark that the prepositions in the verse are separated from the verbs which they ordinarily precede in the non-vedic Sanskrit. The preceptor prays to enter into Bhaga, the Lord and asks him to enter into him (the preceptor) so that he may be washed of all the sins in the thousand forms of the Lord.

यथापःप्रवतायंति । यथामासाअहर्जरं । एवंमांब्रह्मचारिणः । धातरायंतुसर्वतःस्वाहा । प्रतिवेशोसिप्रमाभाहिप्रमापद्यस्व ॥ १२ ॥

यथा, yathâ, as (for example); आप,: âpah, waters, प्रवताः, pravatâḥ, निम्नभूमी, lower grounds or level ; यन्ति, yanti, Go; यथा, yathâ, मासाः, mâsâḥ, months (go to form); अहर्जरम्, aharjaram, अहानि जीर्यन्ति अस्मिन्न इति सवत्सरं a year ; एवं, evam ; मां, mâṃ ; ब्रह्मचारिणः brahmâchariṇaḥ, आयान्तु, âyântu ; धातः dhâtaḥ, preserver of the worlds; आयन्तु, âyantu, let come; सर्वतः, sarvatah from all sides; प्र तिवेशः, prativeśaḥ, श्रमापनयनस्थानं, आसन्नगृहं तादृशः like a resting ground; असि, asi, art, (thou, dhâtaḥ); to me; प्रभाहि, prabhâhi, व्यक्तोभव be clear, open; come to me; मा, mâ, माम् ; प्रपद्यस्व, prapadyasva, take possession of me;

12. Just as waters flow to the low level, just as months go to the year, so may the religious students O! Lord come to me from everywhere ; thou art refuge, enlighten me, reach me.

Commentary.

The preceptor continues his prayer ; he says "just as water flows to the low level or the months come to the year at the end, similarly may the religious students also come to me for the study of the Vedas. O ! Lord thou art a fit refuge, enlighten me and come near me to show favours to me.

भूर्भुवःसुवरितित्राएतास्तिस्रोव्याहृतयः । तासामुहस्मै तांचतुर्थीं । माहचमस्यःप्रवेदयते । महइति । तद्ब्रह्म । सआत्मा ।।अंगान्यन्यादेवताः ।। १३ ।।

भूः bhûḥ, भुवः bhuvaḥ, सुवः suvaḥ, इति iti, वा vâ, एता etâh, these, तिस्रः tisrah three; व्याहृतय : vyâhṛitayaḥ, विशेषेण आहरन्तिविष्णुं भक्तं प्रति, sacred interjections ; तासाम् tasam ; of them ; उहस्म uhasma निपातसमुदायःतस्मिन् in that group ; एताम् etâm, this महाव्याहृतिम् ; चतुर्थीम् chaturthîm, fourth; माहाचमस्यः mâhâchamasyah स्वाहा : प्रवेदयते, pravedayate, teaches ; महः : इति mahaḥ iti, called महः : (the fourth व्याहृति) ; तद् tad, that ; ब्रह्म , brahma, सः saḥ ; आत्मा âtmâ ; अंगानि amgâni limbs, parts ; अन्या anyâ , other ; देवता devatâḥ, deities.

13. Bhuḥ, Bhuvaḥ and Suvaḥ are the three mystic syllables ; of these there is ccertainly the fourth which the son of Mahachamasa instructs as 'great.' It is Brahma ; it is self : the other deities are his (its) bodily parts.

Commentary.

The verse lays down the three *vyahritis* for the instruction of a pupil. They are the different manifested forms of the Lord *viz.*, Pradyumna, Aniruddha and Saṃkaṛṣaṇa. The fourth Vayâhriti called 'the great' is Brahma or Vâsudeva. He is the universal self, the other gods namely Pradyumna &c., are his bodily parts.

भूरितिवाअयंलोकः । भुवइत्यंतरिक्षं । सुवरित्यसौलोकः । महइत्यादित्यः । आदित्येनवावसर्वेलोकामहीयंते । भूरितिवाअग्निः । भुवइतिवायुः । सुवरित्यादित्यः । महइतिचंद्रमाः । चंद्रमसावावसर्वाणिज्योतींषिमहीयंते । भूरितिवाऋचः । भुवइतिसामानि । सुवरितियजूंषि । महइतिब्रह्म । ब्रह्मणावावसर्वेवेदामहीयंते । भूरितिवैप्राणः । भुवइत्यपानः । सुवरितिव्यानः । महइत्यन्नं । अन्नेनावावसर्वेप्राणामहीयंते । तावाएताश्चतस्रश्चतुर्धा । चतस्रश्चतस्रोव्याहृतयः । तायोवेद । सवेदब्रह्म । सर्वस्मैदेयाबलिमावहंति ॥ १४ ॥

भूः bhûḥ ; इति iti ; भूः इति that which is called भूः ; अयम् ayam, this ; लोकः lokaḥ, world. The God in the form of this world ; भुव : bhûvaḥ ; इतिः iti भुव : इति that called bhuvaḥ. अन्तरिक्ष antarikṣaṃ, the sky that form of God in that place called by that name ; सुवः suvah ; सुवरिति that which is called suvaḥ ; असौ asau, that, other heavenly region and the god existing in it assuming that name ; महः mahaḥ इति iti महः : इति that called mahaḥ ; आदित्यः âdityaḥ, the sun, that form of god in it ; आदित्येन âdityena, by the sun, by the god in it. वाव vâva किल surely ; सर्वे sarve, all ; लोकाः lokâḥ, worlds (so called things) ; महीयन्ते mahiyante, पूज्यन्ते are revered, are magnified ; भू : bhûḥ, इति iti, वा vâ, अग्नि, agniḥ, the god in the form of fire ; भुव ; bhuvaḥ इति iti, वायु : vûyuḥ the god in the wind ; सुवः suvah, इति itê, आदित्य : adityaḥ, the sun. ; महः mahaḥ, इति itê, चन्द्रमाः chandramâḥ, the moon ; चन्द्रमसा, chandramasâ, by the moon (the god in moon) ; वाव vâva, सर्वाणि sarvaṇî all. ज्योतींषि jyotîṃṣi, तत्स्थानितन्नामकानि देवरूपाणि the heavenly lights and the forms of god in those lights ; भूव bhûḥ, इति itê ऋच : ṛichaḥ, ऋग्वेदनामा : तत्स्थ : तन्नामापरमेश्वर : Rik verses and the god assuming that name and residing in them, भुवः, bhuvaḥ इति itî, सामानि sâmâni, sâma verses, also the god in them, सुवः suvaḥ इति ite, यजूंषि yajûṃsi, the yajurveda verses. The form of god in them ; महः इति ब्रह्म mahaḥ iti brahmà, ब्रह्मणा, वाव, सर्वे, वेदाः महीयन्ते brahmaṇâ vâva, sarve, vedâḥ, mahîyante ; भूःइति वै आपः bhûḥ, iti vai, âpâḥ ; अपानः apânaḥ, the wind passing downwards, the god in it; व्यान vyânaḥ, the wind circulating through the whole of the body and the form of god exhibited by it ; मह mahaḥ इति iti, अन्नम् annam, अन्नेन वाव सर्वे प्राणा महीयन्ते ; ताः tâḥ, those, भूः भुवः सुवः महः इति वा iti vâ इति अत्र निर्दिष्टाः stated here ; एताः etâḥ चतस्रः chatasraḥ four ; चतुर्धा chaturdhâ, four times in four ways. i e. each vyâhritih भूः has four functions 1., about worlds, 2., about heavenly brilliant lights, 3., about the Vedas and knowledge 4., about the lives and winds that manifest them ; चतस्रः चतस्रः chatasrāḥ chatasraḥ, four into four, sixteen ; व्याहृतयः vyâhṛitayaḥ भगवन्मूर्तयः particular forms or manifestations of God. ताः tâḥ, यः yâḥ, वेद veda, knows; सः वेद saḥ veda, ब्रह्म brahma सर्वस्मै देवाः sarvasmai devah; सर्वे देवाः sarve devâḥ all gods; बलिम् balim पूजाम् things offered in adoration of ब्रह्म Viṣṇu.

14. 'Bhu' is certainly this world; 'Bhuva' is the intervening space ; Suva is the yonder world. 'Mahas' is the sun; by the sun certainly are all the regions glorified. 'Bhu' is certainly fire ; 'Bhuva' is air. 'Suva' is sun ; 'Mahas' is moon : by the moon certainly all the lights are glorified. 'Bhu' is the *rik*, 'Bhuva' is, 'Sâma ;' 'Suva' is Yajus. Mahas is Brahma, by Brahma certainly all the Vedas are glorified. 'Bhu' is vital air ; 'Bhuva' is foul air ; 'Suva' is the air that pervades the whole bodily system ; 'Mahas' is food : by the food certainly all the vital airs are glorified. All these four are four-fold ; the vyâhritis are four, four ; one who knows them, knows Brahma. All the gods bring offering to him.

Commentary.

Here in the present verse, we have four vyâhritis which are four mystic syllables, represented by regions, lights, the Veda and vital air Aniruddha one of the four forms of the Lord pervades terrestrial region ; Pradyumna the second manifested form of the Lord pervades the intervening space ; Samkarśana the third form pervades the heaven. Vâsudeva pervades the sun. By means of the pervasion of the Lord, all these regions are glorified or worshipped *i. e.*. they rise in the esteem of the people. Fire represents Aniruddha, air represents Pradyumna, the sun represents Saṃkarṣaṇa ; Moon represents Vâsudeva. The rest is the same as above. Now as to the third form of the Lord *viz.*, Saṃkarṣaṇa ; Rik represents Aniruddha in the Saṃkarṣaṇa group ; Sâma represents Pradyumna; Yajus represents Saṃkarṣaṇa ; Brahma represents Vâsudeva. The rest is the same as above. Now as to the fourth group represented by Vâsudeva ; the Prâṇa represents Aniruddha, Apâṇa represents Pradyumna ; Vyâna rep resents Saṃkarṣaṇa ; (Anna) food represents Vâsudeva. The rest is the same as before. Thus we have four divisions of the Vyúha distributed into four different forms of the Vyâhritis. These are, therefore fourfold four *i.e.*, sixteen forms of the Lord. He who understand these forms *i.e.*, worships them, knows Viṣṇu ; all the gods make an offering to such a liberated soul.

यसएषोंतर्हृदयआकाशः । तस्मिन्नयंपुरुषोमनोमयः । अमृतोहिरण्मयः। अंतरेणतालुके। यएषस्तनइवावलंबते । सेंद्रयोनिः । यत्रासौकेशांतोविवर्तते । व्यपोह्यशीर्ष कपाल ॥ १५ ॥

सः saḥ; यः yaḥ; एषः eṣaḥ, this; अन्तः antaḥ, inside ; हृदये hridaye in the heart ; आकाशः âkâśaḥ, space ; तस्मिन् tasmin (आकाशे) in that (space); अयम् ayam, this; भूःनामा पुरुषः puruṣaḥ, the person; मनोमयः manomayaḥ; ज्ञानप्रचुरः as mind, full of the knowing powers of the mind ; अमृतः amritaḥ, नित्यः constant ; हिरण्मयः hiraṇmayaḥ, विलक्षणानन्दप्रचुरः golden, full of extraordinary joy. अन्तरेण तालुके antareṇa taluke तालुकयोः मध्ये between the two pâlates ; यः yaḥ, एषः eṣah, तनः tanaḥ स्तनः nipple, इव, अवलम्बते avalambate, hangs ; सा sâ, that; इन्द्र Indra, इन्द्रनामा ईश्वरः परमेश्वरः; योनि, yoniḥ, स्थानम् place ; यत्र yatra, where; (तत्र) at the roots of hair; असौ asau, that; (केशान्तः) keśḥntaḥ ; केशमूलम् केशान्तः keśantaḥ, केशमूलम् the end of hair. the roct of hair ; वि vi (without the case termination; विःसुपर्णारूपः संकर्षणः, that supreme form of god; वर्तते vartate exists ; व्यपः vyapaḥ, वासुदेवः God ; हि hi, evidently ; अशीर्षकपाले âśîrṣkapâle ; शिरः कपालान्यदेशे ; कपालादुपरियावत्, kapâladupariyâvat, just between the forehead and head ; (वर्तते व्यपः)

15. There is ether inside the heart; in it there is *puruṣa* all-intelligence, immortal, golden. Between the two palates, there is (uvula) which hangs like a nipple; it is the seat of Indra. There exists the root of hair after separating the two parietal bones of the skull.

Commentary.

The well known cardiac ether or space which is inside that heart, is pervaded by Aniruddha, who is here called *purusa*; he is all intelligence, immortal and happiness. The space in the palatial region within the mouth is called uvula; it hangs like a nipple and is the seat of Pradyumna. Where there is root of the hair, there exists (*vi*) the eagle representing Saṃkarṣaṇa. Where the parietal bones join, there exists Vâsudeva. The scholiast separates '*vi.*,' from 'vartate' and takes it in the sense of eagle who is the carrier of Viṣṇu; he derives 'Vyapohya' very curiously from 'Vyapah' meaning Vâsudeva. Vâsudeva exists even after the dissolution of the worlds; 'hi' means certainly. He separates 'a,' connects it with 'śirṣakapâla' and reads it as 'aśirskapala' meaning any region other than cranial.

भूरित्यग्नौप्रतितिष्ठति । भुवइतिवायौ । सुवरित्यादित्ये महइतिब्रह्मणि । आप्नोतिस्वाराज्यं । आप्नोतिमनसस्पतिं । वाकपतिश्चक्षुष्पतिः । श्रोत्रपतिर्विज्ञानपतिः । एतत्ततो भवति ॥ १६ ॥

भूः bhûḥ; इति iti; अग्नौ agnau, in fire; प्रतितिष्ठति pratitiṣthati, resides; that god भूः resides in agni; भुवः bhuvaḥ; इति iti; वायौ vâyau; in the wind; सुवः suvaḥ; इति iti; आदित्ये âditye, in the wind; महः mahaḥ; इति iti; ब्रह्मणि brahmaṇi, in Brahma; आप्नोति apnoti; व्याप्नोति occupies, pervades through; स्वाराज्यम् swarâjyam; जगत् the world; आप्नोति apnoti; मनसस्पतिम् manasaspatim; the lord of mind, god; वाक्पतिः vâkpatih; तन्नियन्ताः tanniyantâḥ; the lord of speech residing in the tongue; चक्षुष्पतिः chakṣuṣpatiḥ; the lord of sight residing in eyes; श्रोत्रपति śrotrapatiḥ, the lord of hearing residing in the ears; विज्ञानपतिः vijnânapatih, the lord of knowledge residing in beings; एतत् etat, this; ततः tataḥ, through him by him, भवति bhavati, becomes; he becomes all this

(the ruler of actions and the resident of the organs working.)

16. 'Bhû' he resides in fire ; 'Bhuvah' he resides in air ; 'Suva' he resides in the Sun; 'Maha' he resides in Brahma; he obtains the kingdom of self ; he obtains the lordship of mind. Lord of voice, lord of sight, lord of hearing, lord of knowledge, he thereby becomes.

Commentary

Aniruddha resides in fire as represented by the monosyllable 'Bhû'. Pradyumna resides in air represented by Bhuva ; Saṃkarsaṇa resides in sun as represented by 'Suva', Vâsudeva resides in Brahmâ as represented by 'Maha'; he resides there as pervading the universe. He becomes lord of the mind *i.e.*, he obtains Aniruddha. He pervades himself and the whole universe. He becomes the controller of speech, sight, hearing and knowledge.

आकाशशरीरंब्रह्म । सत्यात्मप्राणारामंमनआनंदं । शांतिसमृद्धममृतं । इतिप्राचीनयोग्योपास्व ॥ १७ ॥

आकाशशरीरम् âkâśa sariram, आकाशवद् व्याप्यदेहं, occupying the body like ether ; ब्रह्म brahma ; सत्यात्म satyâtma, साधुगुणपूर्ण, full of saintly qualities ; प्राणाराम prâṇârâmaṃ, sporting in the vicinity of praṇas as they are strengthening and comforting : मनः आनन्दम् manah ânandam ; ज्ञानानन्दात्मकं jñânânandâtmakaṃ, giving happiness to be derived through knowldge; शान्ति समृद्धम् śânti samridham; rich in peace ; अमृतं amṛitam; नित्यं not dying, deathless ; इति iti, means as mentioned above ; प्राचीन योग्य prâchîn yogya चतुर्मुख chaturmukha, O ! worthy of the ancients, O ! Brahmadeva ; उपास्व upâsva worship, praise ; The God Viṣṇu addressed thus to the God Brahmâ.

17. O! Worthy of the ancients, worship Brahma whose body is ether, whose soul is truth, whose vital air is enjoyment, whose mind is happiness who is perfect peace and immortal.

Commentary.

Brahma is Vâsudeva ; he pervades the whole universe like ether; he is full of good qualities; he is the garden or sporting place of air *i.e.* he is powerful and happy ; he is both intelligence and happiness; he is perfect peace by reason of the increase of happiness; he is perfect in himself though possessed of corporeal body, he is immortal. O! Brahmâ, the foremost amongst the devotees, worship such Brahma" says Vishnu to Brahmâ.

पृथिव्यंतरिक्षं द्यौर्दिशोवांतरदिशाः । अग्निर्वायुरादित्य-
श्चंद्रमानक्षत्राणि । आपओषधयोवनस्पतय आकाशआत्मा ।
इत्यधिभूतं । अथाध्यात्मं । प्राणोव्यानोपानउदानः समानः
चक्षुः श्रोत्रंमनोवाक्त्वक् । चर्ममाँसँस्नावास्थिमज्जा ।
एतदधिविधायऋषिरवोचत् । पाङ्क्तंवाइदँसर्वं । पाङ्क्तेनै
वपाङ्क्तं स्पृणोतीति ॥ १८ ॥

पृथिवी prithivî, earth; अन्तरिक्षम् ântarikṣam, intervening space; द्यौ: dyauḥ, heaven ; दिश: diśaḥ, directions ; अन्तरदिशा: antaradiṣâḥ, inter-directions, corners ; अग्नि: वायु: आदित्य: चन्द्रमा: âgniḥ, vâyuḥ, âdityaḥ, chandramâḥ, नक्षत्राणि nakṣatsâṇi, stars ; आप: âpaḥ, water; ओषधय: oṣadhayaḥ, medicinal herbs, trees and plants ; वनस्पतय: vanaspatayaḥ, the lord of forests, big trees and creepers ; आकाश: âkâśaḥ, ether; आत्मा âtmâ, soul; इति iti, अधिभूतम् âdhibhûtam, microcosmic ; अथ atha, अध्यात्मम adhyât-mam, physiological ; प्राण: prâṇaḥ ; व्यान: vyanaḥ, अपान: âpânaḥ, उदान: udânaḥ, the wind occupying the throat ; समान: samânaḥ, the wind near the navel ; चक्षु: chakṣuḥ, eye ; श्रोत्रम् śrotram, ear ; मन: manaḥ mind ; वाक् vâk, speech, त्वक् tvak, the organ of touch; चर्म charma, skin ; मांसम् mâṃsam, flesh ; स्नाव snâva, muscle ; अस्थि asthi, bones ; मज्जा majjâ, marrow ; एतत् etat, पृथिव्यादिपञ्चषटकम् the group of the six of the five primary elements ; अधिविधाय adhividhâya, अधिकृत्य having ruled over (those) or described, stated (these) ; ऋषि: ṛiṣiḥ, विष्णु: ; अवोचत् avochat, spoke, said ; पांक्तम् pânktam, property of beings classed in five or group of five ; वै, vai, certainly ; इदम् idam, this ; सर्वम् sarvam, all ; पांक्तेन pâṃktena, with the help of this group of fives ; पांक्तम् pâṃktam, स्पृणोति spriṇoti, strengthens, completes, enables to do work ; इति, iti, this, the last sentence which is said by Viṣṇu.

18. The Earth, intervening space, heaven, quarters, the corners; fire, air, soul, the moon, stars ; water, vegetables, herbs, ether, soul; this is micro-cosmic aspect. Now as regards physiological aspect ; vital air pervading the whole body, filthy air, air pervading throat; air pervading umbilical region; the eye, ear, mind, tongue and touch ; the skin, flesh, nerve, bone, marrow.

Having described this, the seer said " the whole of it is made of five ; by means of five, he strengthens five. "

Commentary.

In this verse, we have two aspects, microcosmic and physiological; each of them consists of three sets of five manifested forms of the Lord, *viz*, Nârâyaṇa, Aniruddha, Pradyumna, Saṃkarṣaṇa and Vâsudeva. Having described the two aspects, the seer of the Veda comes to the conclusion that the whole universe is composed of five ingredients. It is by means of the five-fold manifested form of the Lord that he makes the earth &c., five in number fit for the discharge of their duties.

ओमितिब्रह्म । ओमितीदँ सर्वं । ओमित्येतदनुकृतिहस्मवाअप्योश्रावयंति । ओमितिसामानिगायंति । ओँशोमितिशस्त्राणिशँसंति । ओमित्यध्वर्युःप्रतिगरंप्रतिगृणाति । ओमितिब्रह्माप्रसौति । ओमित्यग्निहोत्रमनुजानाति । ओमितिब्राह्मणःप्रवक्ष्यन्नाहब्रह्मोपाप्नवानीति । ब्रह्मैवोपाप्नोति ॥१६॥

ओमिति omiti, what is called, ब्रह्म is called ओमिति om ; इदम् सर्वं idam sarvaṃ, all this (creation) ; ओमिति omiti, एतत् etat, om; अनुकृति anukriti, imitation, copy ; हस्मवै hasmavai, evidently true ; अपि api, also ; ओ स्रावय इति आश्रावयन्ति O śrâvaya iti âśrâvayanti, ओं अधिकोच्च होतृस्थविष्णो ! श्रावय स्वमूलरूपं श्रावय इति । आश्रावयंन्ति उच्चैरुच्चारयंति । अध्वर्यव: होतृस्थं प्रति इत्यर्थः । ओं O ! Viṣṇu residing in the sacrificer ; श्रावय śrâvaya, say to us your original (correct) form ; इति, iti. thus, (आश्रवय इति) आश्रवयति âśravayati, cry loudly (the sacrificial head priests to Viṣnu in the sacrificer's body, ओ इति एतद् ओंकारानुकरणरूपं प्रसिद्धं इति भाव:, the substance is that every thing follows ओम्, or imitates ओम् as for example, ओ is the well known attempt of imitating ओम् ; ओमिति omiti, saying om in the beginning, thereby meaning that after addressing Viṣṇu as Om ; सामानि sâmâni, Sâma verses ; गायन्ति gâyanti, they sing (to or addressing Visṇu); ओम्, शोमिति om śomiti, ओ शं इतिओं अत्युच्चसुखविष्णो अवरक्ष इति "O ! great happiness-giver Viṣṇu protect " like this, beginning with calling om ; शास्त्राणि śâstrâṇi, the praising hymns ; शंसन्ति śaṃsanti, praise ; ओमिति omiti, ओ अधिकोच्चमहाधाम इति addressing Viṣṇu ; अध्वर्यु: adhvaryuḥ, ऋत्विग्विशेष: the sacrificial priest ; प्रतिगरम् pratigaram, a verse ; प्रतिगृणाति pratigriṇâti, उच्चारयति says ; ओमिति omiti, addresing Viṣṇu ; ब्रह्मा brahmâ, the priest acting the part of Brahmâ ; प्रसौति prasauti, सोममभिषुणोति extracts soma juice ; ओमिति omiti, receiving orders from Viṣṇu ; अग्निहोत्रम् Agnihotram, the offering of oblations to fire, and the worship of fire ; अनुजानाति anujânâti, gets permission (when he says Om ;) ओमिति ब्राह्मणः प्रवक्ष्यन् आह ब्रह्म उपाप्नवानि इति construction :—प्रवक्ष्यन् ब्राह्मणः (स्वं प्रति) ब्रह्म उपाप्नवानि इति (मत्वा) ओमिति आह; प्रवक्ष्यन् pravakṣyan, one studying the Vedic religion and philosopical books ; ब्राह्मणः brâhmaṇaḥ, a Brahmin student ; ब्रह्म उपाप्नवानि upâpnavâni, that he would get ; इति·ब्रह्म उपाप्नवानि the idea of getting Viṣṇu ओमिति omiti आह, â ı a, says ; the meaning of the verse is that a Brahmin student of the Vedas says Om (Viṣṇu) in order that he would obtain Viṣṇu ; ब्रह्म Brahma, एव eva, आप्नोति âpnoti, he gets Brahma.

19. 'Om' is Brahma; Om is the entire universe. 'Om' is certainly a copy; also when 'speak aloud' is utttered they cry aloud; the singers sing songs with Om; 'Om' 'Som', they recite prose verses. 'Om', the Adhwaryu utters words of encouragement. 'Om', the Brahmâ priest extracts soma juice ; 'Om' he orders Agnihottra. 'Om' he says, when desirous of performing a sacrifice 'may I obtain Brahma'; he obtains Brahma,

Commentary,

Om is Viṣṇu; it is the name of Viṣṇu. Every one who is desirous of performing a Vedic rite utters 'Om' in the beginning when any mantra is uttered loudly. 'Om' is uttered first. The singers of the Sâma songs called Udgâtri priests sing them with 'Om'. To the Udgâtri class belong Prastotâ, Pratihartâ, Subrahmaṇya and Udgâ tri. The Hotri group consists of Hotâ, Maitrâvaruṇa, Acchâvâka and Grâvastut. 'Om' is uttered when they recite the prose songs. The Adwaryu priest signifies his assent by reciting *pratigara* Mantra. The Hotâ obtains the permission of the Adhwaryu to sing prose songs ; he gives his assent which is called *pratigara.* The Brahmâ priest extracts soma juice by invoking Viṣṇu. The sacrificer also permits his priest to commence the Agnihottra by uttering. 'Om,' He who wishes to perform the Brâhma sacrifice also commences by uttering 'Om' and saying 'may I obtain Brahma.' He obtains Brahma if he performs the various parts of the ceremoney systematically.

ऋतंचस्वाध्यायप्रवचनेच । सत्यंचस्वाध्यायप्रवचनेच । तपश्चस्वाध्यायप्रवचनेच । दमश्चस्वाध्यायप्रवचनेच । शमश्च स्वाध्यायप्रवचनेच । अग्नयश्चस्वाध्यायप्रवचनेच । अग्निहोत्रंचस्वाध्यायप्रवचनेच । अतिथयश्चस्वाध्यायप्रवचनेच । मानुषंचस्वाध्यायप्रवचनेच । प्रजाच स्वाध्यायप्रवचनेच । प्रजनश्चस्वाध्यायप्रवचनेच । प्रजातिश्चस्वाध्यायप्रवचनेच ॥ २० ॥

ऋतम् ṛitam, यथार्थज्ञानं the virtue of knowing a thing rightly. Right knowledge स्वाध्याय: swâdhâyaḥ, receiving of lessons; प्रवचनम् pravachanam, lecture, discourse; satyaṃ यथार्थज्ञानपूर्वकं वचनं, तत्पूर्वकं करणंच saying and doing of a thing after knowing its real nature (what it actually is) truthfulness; तप: tapaḥ, ध्यानं, सत्य पूज्यपूजाच तप: meditation and worship of God; दम: damah, इंद्रियनिग्रह: control of the senses; शम: śamaḥ भगवन्निष्ठा devotion to God; अग्नय: agnayaḥ, अग्नीनां आधानम् keeping office; अग्निहोत्रम् agnihotram, the performance of sacrificiad rites; अतिथय: atithayaḥ, अतिथिपूजा: the hospitality to be shown to (unexpected or expected) guests; मानुष्यम् mânuṣam, मनुष्यसंबंधिधर्म प्रदर्शनम् performance of one's duties towards humanity; प्रजा prajâ, progeny, offspring, प्रजनम् prajanam; bringing up and protection of children; प्रजाति: prajâtiḥ, पित्रा पुत्रस्य, The giving of special name and the initiation of the son by his father; now all these virtues and acts are as necessary as study and lectures. One must therefore pay as much attention to the imparting of education as he must do to those good things,

20. Right, study and teaching; truth, study and teaching; penance, study and teaching; control of senses, study and teaching; peace, study and teaching; fire, study and teaching; Agnihottra, study and teaching; (attendance on) guests, study and teaching; humanity, study and teaching; offspring, study and teaching; procreation, study and teaching; birth, study and teaching.

Commentary.

The duties that have been cast upon one who is desirous of the Vedic study are that he must study the Vedas, teach them to the religious students throughout his life along with other duties of life; he must be righteous and truthful. He should control his senses and should devote himself to the service of the Lord. He should establish fire, perform Agnihottra, receive religious guests and perform th duties of a man. He should produce children and bring them up.

सत्यमितिसत्यवचाराथीतरः । तपइतितपोनित्यःपौरुशिष्टिः । स्वाध्यायप्रवचनेएवेतिनाकोमौद्गल्यः । तद्धितपस्तद्धि तपः ॥ २१ ॥

सत्यवचाः satyavachâh, truth-speaker ; राथीतरः râthîtarah, some one named Rathitarah ; सत्यमिति satyamiti, सत्यं श्रेय इति आह said that truthfulness was superior to others ; तपोनित्यः पौरुशिष्टिः तप इति; तपोनित्यः taponityah, well practised in meditation and worship of god ; पौरुशिष्टिः paurusistih, the sage called by the name ; तपः इति tapah iti, said that meditation and worship must be preferred to the rest ; मौद्गल्यः maudgalyah, मुद्गलपुत्रः the son of Mudgala ; नाकः nâkah, called by that name ; स्वाध्यायप्रवचने एव इति svâdhyâyapravachane eva iti, said that study and lectures alone were the best of all; तद्धि taddhi, because that (is) ; तपः tapah, penance; तद्धि surely that is ; तपः, study and lectures as they deal only with God and as God possesses all the virtues and does every thing : the time devoted to the knowledge about him through the scriptures is, as it were, given to all the virtues and actions.

21. The truthful son of Rathitara says ' truth '; the son of Purusista devoted to penance says ' penance' ; Nâka son of Mudgala says " study and teaching only." Therefore certainly penance, therefore certainly penance.

Commentary.

The verse describes the different views of the sages. The son of Rathitara attaches greatest importance to truth ; the son of Purusisti is of opinion that the penance is best of all. Nâka son of Mudgala holds that the study and teaching of the Vedas are most essential. Having set forth the different views, the verse concludes by saying that the austerities are most important of all.

अहंवृक्षस्यरेरिवा । कीर्तिःपृष्ठंगिरेरिव । उर्ध्वपवित्रोवाजिनी

वस्वमृतमसि । द्रविणँ सवर्चसं । सुमेधाअमृतोच्चितः ।
इतित्रिशंकोर्वेदानुवचनं ॥ २२ ॥

अहं ahaṃ ; संसारवृक्षस्य, samsâra vrikṣasya, of the tree of worldly movements ; रेरिवा rerivâ, छेत्ता cutter ; कीर्तिः kîrtiḥ, (my) fame ; गिरेः gireḥ, of a mountain ; पृष्ठम्, pristham, the surface ; इव, Iva, like ; विस्तीर्णः: vistîrṇaḥ, spread over, ऊर्ध्वपवित्रः ûrdhvapavıtraḥ, हरिणा पावितः purified by Hari (God) who is up ; वाजिनीवसुअमृते vâjinî vasu amritam, तेनवाजिनीवसुना अमृतः (प्रारब्धकर्मनिष्ठ'कः) अस्मि, I am free from my former karma through the favour of the god who is in the sun ; वाजिनी vâjinî, the sun ; वाजिनीवसुः vâjinivasuḥ, वाजिन्यां सूर्येवसति इति; that which resides in the sun (the god therein) ; द्रविणम् (इव) सर्वचसम् ; द्रविणम् Draviṇem, gold ; सवचर्सम् savarchasam, brilliant without any impurity ; सुमेधा, (अस्मि) sumedhâ, (asmi), I am sumedhâ, of good understanding or power; I am अमृतोच्चितः amritokṣitaḥ, अमृतेन विष्णुना उच्चितः सिक्तः व्याप्नोः वा ; I am full of God ; इति iti, the above; त्रिशंकोः: triśamkoḥ, of (by) Triśanku, of the king named thus ; वेदानुवचनम् vedânuvachanam, the interpretation of the Vedas.

22. I am the cutter of the tree glorious like the top of a mountain ; I am purified by one above, I am made immortal by the pervader in the sun. I am bright gold, I am intelligence and sprinkled with immortalitly. This is the fruit of the Vedic teaching by Trisanku.

Commentary.

The world is compared to a tree. See Bhagavadgitâ XV. 1.; Katha VI. I. The tree referred to is Aśvattha which means 'which is not to last till tomorrow'. The world which we live in, is temporary and illusory; it can be destroyed by spiritual knowledge. Some one who has reached the highest stage in the spiritual knowledge says that he has destroyed the world by the spiritual knowledge ; that his fame has spread throughout the length breadth of the world ; that he has been sanctified by Hari who is above all; that he has been made immortal by Viṣṇu who pervades the sun ; that he has become brilliant gold *i.e.,* happiness personified ; that he is intelligence and has been sprinkled over with nectar : this is the result of the teaching of Triśanku.

वेदमनूच्याचार्योंतेवासिनमनुशास्ति। सत्यंवद । धर्मंचर । स्वाध्यायान्माप्रमदः । आचार्यायप्रियंधनमाहृत्यप्रजातंतुंमा व्यवच्छेत्सीः । सत्यान्नप्रमदितव्यं । धर्मान्नप्रमदितव्यं । कुशलान्नप्रमदितव्यं । भूत्यैनप्रमदितव्यं । स्वाध्यायप्रवचनाभ्यांनप्रमदिव्यं । देवपितृकार्याभ्यांनप्रमदितव्यं । मातृदेवोभव । पितृदेवोभव । आचार्यदेवोभव । अतिथिदेवोभव । यान्यनवद्यानिकर्माणि । तानिसेवितव्यानि । नोइतराणि । यान्यस्माकँसुचरितानि । तानित्वयोपास्यानि । नोइतराणि । येकेचास्मच्छ्रेयाँसोब्राह्मणाः । तेषांत्वयासनेनप्रश्वसितव्यं । श्रद्धयादेयं । अश्रद्धयादेयं । श्रियादेयं । ह्रियादेयं । भियादेयं । संविदादेयं ॥ २३ ॥

वेदम् vedam ; अनूच्य anûchya, व्याख्याय, after lecturing on ; आचार्यः âchâryaḥ, the preceptor ; अन्तेवासिनम् antevâsinam, शिष्यम्, the pupil ; अनुशास्ति anuśâsti, शिक्षयति, instructs ; सत्यं the truth ; वद vada, speak, tell ; धर्मं dharmaṃ, कर्तव्यं, duty, चर chara, कुरु, do ; स्वाध्यायात् swâdhyâyât, from your study (receiving lessons) ; मा प्रमदः mâ pramadaḥ, प्रमादं माकार्षीः, do not miss, do not forget your lessons and your duty of stndying ; आचार्याय âchâryâya, to the teacher ; प्रियं priyaṃ ; इष्टं, desired, proper by him (the teacher) ; धनम् dhanam, money, as गुरुदक्षिणा, tuition fee ; आहृत्य âhṛitya, आनीय-दत्वा, after bringing and giving (the teacher the tuition fee desired by him) ; प्रजातंतु prajâtaṃtuṃ ; प्रजासंतानम्, the continuation of offspring ; मा व्यवच्छेत्सीः mâ vyavachchhetsîḥ, do not cut off (the line) or stop (the continuation of progeny) ; सत्यात् satyât, from truth ; नप्रमदितव्यम् napramaditavyam, not to go astray ; धर्मात् dharmât, from your duty; नप्रमदितव्यम्, कुशलात् kuaślât, श्रेयोहेतुव्यापारात्, from doing things with a good motive and intention ; भूत्यै bhûtyai, ऐश्वर्यार्थं, in matters of gaining and retaining wealth and prosperity (to be acquired and retained by the virtuous means only) ; स्वाध्यायप्रवचनाभ्यां svâdhyâya pravachanâbhyâm, in matters of revising the studied subjects and thinking over the old lectures and delivering fresh ones ; देवपितृकार्याभ्याम devapitri-karyabhyâm, (not to swerve) from your duties towards your god and your forefathers ; मातृदेवोभव mâtridevobhava, become one who thinks his mother to be his god ; पितृदेवोभव, pitridevobhava, become one who thinks his father as his god ; आचार्यदेवोभव âchâryadevobhava, become one who thinks his teacher as his god. अतिथिदेवोभव Atithi devo bhava, become one who thinks his guest to be his god ; यानि yâni, which (are) अनवद्यानि anavadyâni, अनिन्दितानि ; not censured or not found fault with ; कर्माणि karmâṇi, deeds ; तानि tâni, those ; सेवितव्यानि sevitavyâni, कर्तव्यानि, (are) necessarily to be done (by you) ; नोइतराणि no itarâṇi, not the others ; (सावद्यानि) (deserving censure) ; यानि yâni ; अस्माकम् asmâkam, to us ; सुचरितानि sucharitâni, actions which are good (to us); तानि tâni ; त्वया tvayâ, by thee (by you) ; उपास्यानि upâsyâni, to be properly done ; नो इतराणि no itarâni ; ये के च ye ke cha, whosoever, any persons ; अस्मच्छ्रेयांसः asmachchhreyâṃsaḥ, मत्तः, अपि श्रेष्ठाः, superior even to me (the teacher) ; ब्राह्मणाः brâhmaṇâḥ, brâhmins (or philsophers) professors of the Vedas ; तेषां, teṣâṃ, of those superiors (or them) ; त्वया tvayâ, by you (you) आसनेन, asanena by offering a seat; प्रश्वसितव्यम् praśvasitavyam, you ought to try to remove their fatigues (you ought to refresh them) ; श्रद्धयादेयं śradhayâ deyaṃ, to be given with sincerity ; अश्रद्धया (पि) देयम् aśraddhayâ (pi) deyam, to be given even through insincerity ; अश्रद्धया अदेयम्, not to be given without sincerity ; श्रियादेयम् śriyadeyam, to be given in cheerful mood ; ह्रियादेयम् Hriya- deyam, to be given with modesty ; भियादेयम् bhiyâdeyam, to be given through fear of other people ; संविदादेयम् saṃvidâdeyam, to be given with kindness.

23. Having explained the Vedas the preceptor instructs the resident student. Speak truth; perform thy duty; do not neglect thy study ; after offering the desired wealth to thy preceptor, do not stop the line of issue. Do not be negligent of truth ; do not be careless of duty ; do not be careless of the means of prosperity ; do not be careless to be great ; do not be careless of the study and teaching ; do not neglect the offerings of the gods and manes. Regard thy mother as a goddess ; regard thy father as a god ; regard thy preceptor as thy god ; regard the religious guest as thy god. Follow our acts which are unimpeachable but not other ; regard our good conduct with veneration but not the other. Those who are better versed in the spiritual science than ourselves

should be received by thee by offering them a seat. Make a gift with faith, do not give without faith, give with pleasure, give with humility, give with fear and give with kindness.

Commentary.

The religious preceptor after teaching the Vedas instructs his disciple to observe certain rules which are for guidance in one's life ; he is enjoined to speak truth, to perform his duty, to continue his after-study, to offer voluntary donation not beyond his means to the preceptor and to settle in life in order to propagate the line of succession. He is further told not to neglect truth, duty, the means of prosperity and success in life, reading, teaching and making offerings to the gods and the departed souls. He is commanded to respect his mother, father, preceptor and the religious guest. He is further ordered to follow the good action and conduct of his preceptor but not any evil one ; he is to respect abler men than his preceptor by offering them seats. He is enjoined to be charitable with faith but not without faith ; with cheerful mind, with humility, with fear and with kindness.

अथयदितेकर्मविचिकित्सावावृत्तविचिकित्सावास्यात् । येतत्रब्राह्मणाःसंमर्शिनः । युक्ताआयुक्ताः । अलूक्षाधर्मकामास्युः । यथातेतत्रवर्तेरन् । तथातत्रवर्तेथाः । अथाभ्याख्यातेषुवर्तेथाः । येतत्रब्राह्मणाःसंमर्शिनः । युक्ताः आयुक्ताः । अलूक्षाः धर्मकामास्युः । यथा तेतेषुवर्तेरन् । तथातेषु वर्तेथाः । एषआदेशः । एषउपदेशः । एषावेदोपनिषत् । एतदनुशासनं । एवमुपासितव्यं । एवमुचैतदुपास्यं । शन्नोमित्रः शंवरुणः । शन्नोभवत्वर्यमा । शन्नइंद्रोबृहस्पतिः शन्नोविष्णुरुरुक्रमः । नमोब्रह्मणे । नमस्तेवायो । त्वमेवप्रत्यक्षंब्रह्मासि । त्वामेवप्रत्यक्षंब्रह्मावादिषं । ऋतमवादिषं सत्य मवादिषं । तन्मामावीत् । तद्वक्तारमावीत् । आवीन्मां । आवीद्वक्तारं ।

ॐ शांतिःशांतिः शांतिः ॥२४॥ इतिप्रथमवल्लीसंपूर्णा ॥१॥

अथ atha ; यदि yadi, if ; ते te, thy ; कर्मविचिकित्सा karma vichikitsâ, यज्ञादिभगवदाराधनकर्मसंदेहः, any doubt in the proper performance of the sacrifices or other devotional services ; वृत्तविचिकित्सा vrittavichikitsâ, कर्मांगाचारविषयसंदेहः, any doubt as regards the minute details of any practice, (conduct) ; वा vâ, or ; स्यात् syât, (if there) be; ये तत्र, ye tatra, those there; संमर्शिनः sammarśinaḥ; विमर्शकारिणः, capable of removing doubts; युक्ताः yuktâḥ, accustomed to application to study ; आयुक्ताः âyuktâḥ, persistent in the practise of one's duty and religious rites ; अलूक्षाः alûkṣâḥ, अरूक्षाः प्रश्नेकृतेकोपरहिताः, who do not get displeased or annoynd if they are questioned something ; धर्मकामाः dharmakâmâḥ ; अदृष्टार्थिनः, who are desirous to perform their duty but not anxious to get wealth ; स्युः syuḥ, would be ; यथा yathâ, as, in the manner in which ; ते te, they ; तेषु teṣu, in those matters (about which you have got doubts) ; तथा tathâ, in that manner ; तेषु teṣu, matters ; वर्तेथाः vartethâḥ, behave, practise, do ; एषआदेश eṣa âdeśaḥ, इमामाज्ञांहरेः, this is the message ; उपदेशः upadeśaḥ, advice ; एषा eṣâ, this; वेदोपनिषत् vedopaniṣat, the secret of the Vedas ; एतद् etad, this ; अनुशासनम् anuśâsanam; शिक्षा (special) instruction ; एवम् evam; as is advised before, as regards the course of conduct ; उपासितव्यम् upâsitavyam, to be necessarily done ; एवमुचा evamuchâ, thus ; एतत्, etat, this ; उपास्यम्, upâsyam, to be done.

24. If thou hast any doubt in an act or conduct, act as the thoughtful learned men of the spiritual science, who are regular, devoted, peaceful and dutiful, act. As regards censured acts, act as the thoughtful learned men of spiritual science, who are regular, devoted, peaceful and dutiful, act. This is the message ; this is the advice : this is the secret of the Vedas ; this is the instruction. Thus it is to be acted upon, and thus should it be practised. Om ! let Mitra be favourable to us, let Varuṇa be favourable to us, let Indra and Brihaspati be favourable to us, let Viṣṇu of powerful strides be favourable to us ; let sulatation be to Brahma, let salutation be to thee O ! Vâyu: thou art alone visible Brahma. I spoke of thee as visible Brahma. I spoke right ; I spoke truth. It there fore protected me ; it therefore protected its speaker; it protected me, it protected the speaker. Om ! peace, peace, peace.

Commentary.

The preceptor continues his instruction to the disciple "when I am gone abroad, if there arises any doubt as to certain act or conduct of life as for instance in the service of the Lord or performance of any ceremony, follow the example of those great men in the spiritual science who are regular, devoted, peaceful and dutiful ; if you have any difficulty in understanding the nature of the prohibited acts, follow the great men, because they are the best guides." This is the message, instruction or direction. The verse concludes with the opening part of the first verse with suitable modifications.

End of the first Valli.

Second Valli.

ॐ ॥ सहनाववतु । सहनौभुनक्तु । सहवीर्यंकरवावहै । तेजस्विनावधीतमस्तुमाविद्विषावहै । ॐ शांतिःशांतिः शांतिः ॥ १ ॥

सहनौ अवतु sahnau avatu, आवयोः सन्निधौगताम् । let it (Brahma) come near us both (the pupil and the teacher) simultaneously ; सहनौ भुनक्तु sahanau (bhunaktu), नौ सह एव पालयतु, let Him protect us both together (guard) ; सह वीर्यम् saha vîryam, strength ability ; करवावहै karavâvahai, let us both do ; सहवीर्यम् करवावहै, let us both together be powerful ; sufficiently able (the pupil capable of grasping the lectures and the teacher able to deliver them in the best way). तेजस्विनौ (भवावः) tejasvinau (bhavâvaḥ) अधीतं अस्तु adhîtaṃ astu, अधीतं फलप्रदंभवतु, let whatever is learnt be fruitful (so that it should bring us to light, make us famous). तेजस्विनौ भवावः, let us both be bright ; let whatever is learnt add lustre to both of us. Let our knowledge be bright ; माविद्विषावहै mâvidviṣâvahai, let us not be frightened (in case either of us commits mistakes) ; शान्तिः śântiḥ, peace.

1. Om ! let him protect us (both together); let him nourish us (both) together ; let us (both) show strength ; let our learning be splendid ; let us (both) be not hostile (to each other); Om ! peace, peace, peace.

Commentary.

In order to avert the misfortune that might befall in the course of study, peace is pronounced and the prayer is made to God to protect and maintain both the teacher and the pupil, to make them strong in the pursuit after knowledge, to make the learning retentive and fruitful and to make them act in unison but not in opposition.

ॐ ब्रह्मविदाप्नोतिपरं । तदेषाभ्युक्ता । सत्यंज्ञानमनंतंब्रह्म । योवेदनिहितंगुहायांपरमेव्योमन् । सोश्नुतेसर्वान्कामान्त्सह । ब्रह्मणाविपश्चितेति ॥ २ ॥

ओं om ; ब्रह्मविद् brahmavid, परब्रह्मज्ञानी, one who knows Brahma ; आप्नोति âpnoti, attains ; परम् param, परब्रह्म Brahma ; तद् tad, in support of the previous statement ; एषा eṣâ, this (ऋक्) (which follows) ; अभ्युक्ता, abhyuktâ, is said; सत्यं Satyaṃ, existing ज्ञानम् jñânam, knowing all this variety and difference in the world ; अनन्तम् anantam, -- देशकालगुणापरिच्छिन्नम्, not broken by the efforts of space, time, and quality ; यः yaḥ, who ; वेद veda, knows ; निहितं nihitaṃ, residing ; गुहायां परमे guhâ yâṃ parame, In a very small cavity (of heart) ; व्योमन् vyoman, in the form of space and the gas in it ; सः saḥ ; अश्नुते aśnute, भुक्ते, enjoys ; सर्वान् कामान् sarvân kâmân, स्वयोग्यानि सुखानि, all desired objects of enjoyment ; सह saha, with ; ब्रह्मणा brahmaṇâ, with Brahman ; विपश्चिता vipaśchitâ ; सर्वज्ञेन ब्रह्मणा सह (only) in the company of the all cognisant Brahman. He attains Brahman not only by the mere presence of Brahman near him but by knowing its nature; इति iti.

2. Om ! One who knows Brahma reaches the highest; it is therefore, said, Brahma is truth, knowledge and eternity, He who knows him hidden in the *heart* and the highest sky, attains all desires along with omniscient Brahma.

Commentary.

One who has attained the highest point in the spiritual science, reaches Brahma. The verse refers to a Vedic *rik* which defines Brahma. He is defined as truth which in Sanscrit means 'unchangeable, immutable at all times.' He is all intelligence or knowledge. He is eternal. One who knows him pervading the smallest part as the heart and the biggest expanse as ether, accomplishes his desires in the world and attains Brahma at the end.

तस्माद्वाएतस्मादात्मनआकाशःसंभूतः । आकाशाद्वायुः । वायोरग्निः । अग्नेरापः । अद्भ्यःपृथिवी । पृथिव्याओषधयः । ओषधीभ्योन्नं । अन्नात्पुरुषः ॥ ३ ॥

तस्माद् tasmâd, owing to its being the creator of the universe ; वै vâi ; एतस्माद्, etasmâd, refers to its being known and attained by the ब्रह्मविद्, through its nearer presence; आत्मनः, âtmanaḥ,from Brahma; आकाशः, âkâ śaḥ, the god in it, also ether itself ; संभूतः, saṃbhûtaḥ, derived its origin; आकाशात्, âkâśât, from âkâśa; वायोः, vâyoḥ, from vayu; अग्निः, agnih, अग्नेः agneḥ, from fire or the god in it ; आपः âpaḥ; अद्भ्यः, adbhyah, from waters ; पृथिवी Prithivî, ; पृथिव्याः prithivyah, from the earth ; ओषधयः osadhayaḥ, vegetables or medical herbs ; ओषधीभ्यः oṣadhîbhyaḥ, from vegetables ; अन्नम् annam, food ; अन्नात् annât, from food ; पुरुषः puruṣaḥ, पुरुषः, तदभिमानी जीवः, तदुभयांतर्गतः हरिः । The body, the Jiva in it and the god in both of them. Now from 4 kinds of आकाश, there are four kinds of winds from which are produced four kinds of fires from them four kinds of waters. From them four kinds of earth from which grow four kinds of vegetables whence are obtained 4 kinds of food and from these four kinds of food, compound of body, life and soul or the living persons.

3. From that, from this self certainly proceeded ether; from ether, air ; from air. fire ; from fire, water ; from water earth ; from earth, the vegetable kingdom ; from the vegetable kingdom, cereals ; from cereals, man.

Commentary.

From Brahma as defined in the preceding verse as the highest and the eternal, the whole creation proceeds. Here in the elements, all the four manifested forms of Hari are included. From Brahma proceeds ether ; from ether we have four kinds of air ; from four kinds of air we have four kinds of fire ; from four kinds of fire we have four kinds of water ; from four kinds of water, we have four kinds of earth ; from four kinds of the earth, we have four kinds of vegetable kingdom ; from four kinds of vegetable kingdom, we have four kinds of cereals, from four kinds of cereals, we have the corporate soul.

सवाएषपुरुषोन्नरसमयः । तस्येदमेवशिरः । अयंदक्षिणः

पक्षः । अयमुत्तरःपक्षः । अयमुत्तरःपक्षः । अयमात्मा । इदंपुच्छ प्रतिष्ठा ॥ ४ ॥

सः, वै, एषः, पुरुषः, saḥ, vai, eṣaḥ, puruṣaḥ; सर्वभूतमूलकारणं, sarvabhûta-mûla kâraṇam, the origin of all the primary great elements ; एषः eṣaḥ, who is called by the names ; आकाशः, पृथिवी, पुरुषः puruṣaḥ, जीवदेहस्थः पुरुषनामा हरिः, God in the person ; अन्नरसमयः annarasa mayaḥ, अन्नरसप्र ुरः, full of the essence of food ; तस्य tasya, of that God in the Jiva ; इदम् idam, this ; एव eva, very (which you see) ; शिरः śiraḥ, head ; अयं ayaṃ, this ; दक्षिणः dakṣiṇaḥ, right ; पक्षः pakṣaḥ, side, arm ; अयम् ayam ; उत्तरः uttaraḥ, left ; पक्षः pakṣaḥ ; अयम् ayam ; आत्मा âtmâ, मध्यदेह जीवदेहः तस्य मध्यदेहः, This soul which is the internal body or life is also His internal body *i.e.*, in this very soul there exists the soul of the person (God in the person) , इदं idaṃ पुच्छम् puchchham, this trunk; प्रतिष्ठा pratiṣṭhâ, feet ; प्रतितिष्ठिति आभ्यामिति, (by which he is enabled to stand) all the organs of the body are controlled by the respective organs of God in it.

4. This certainly is the puruṣa full of the essence of food. This belonging to him is head; it is the southern wing ; it is the northern wing ; it is the (middle part of) body (âtmâ) ; it is the tail, the basis

Commentary.

The verse proceeds to describe the pervasion of Hari in different parts of the body ; Purusa who is pervading the body is Hari and is made up of the essence of food. There are five kośas (cases) called Anna, Prâṇa, Mana, Vijñâña and Ânanda. It is the descr iption of the first kośâ pervaded by Aniruddha. The human head is his head ; the left hand is his southern wing and the right hand is his northern wing ; the middle part of the human body from the neck down to the umblical region is the middle part of his body. The feet which are as it were the foundation are his tail. According to Sâyana the simile is taken from the altar which is constructed inthe form of a falcon in a ceremony of Agnichayana (piling of fire).

तदप्येषश्लोकोभवति ॥ अन्नाद्वैप्रजाःप्रजायंते । याःकाश्च पृथिवीँश्रिताः । अथोअन्नेनैवजीवंति । अथैनदपियंत्यंततः । अन्नँहिभूतानांज्येष्ठं । तस्मात्सर्वौषधमुच्यते । सर्वंवैतेन्नमाप्नुवंति । येन्नंब्रह्मोपास्ते । अन्नँहिभूतानांज्येष्ठं । तस्मात्सर्वौषधमुच्यते । अन्नाद्भूतानिजायंते । जातान्यन्नेनवर्धंते । अद्यतेत्तिचभूतानि । तस्मादन्नंतदुच्यतइति ॥ ५ ॥

तत् tat तत्र in connection with that (the above statement), as an authority or explanation to the above; अपि, also ; श्लोकः ślokaḥ, verse ; भवति bhavati, is ; अन्नात् ennât, from food ; वै vai, certainly ; प्रजाः prajah, created being ; प्रजायंते prajâyante, are born ; याः काश्च yâḥ, kâścha, whichever ; पृथिवीश्रिताः prithivimśritâḥ, on the earth or to the earth ; श्रिताः śritâḥ, live on, or resort to or get support from ; अथ atha, now, अन्नेन annena, by the use of food ; एव eva, only ; जीवंति jivanti, live (after they are born, by the help of the body) ; अथ atha, afterwards at the time of dissolution ; एनत् enat, this food ; God existing in the juice of food) ; अपियंति, apiyanti, enter into the jivas again, returned to the food (God) ; अंततः antataḥ, ultimately ; अन्नं annam, God in food ; हि hi, because ; भूतानांज्येष्ठं bhutânam jyeṣṭham, greater (older) than the beings therein ; तस्मात् tasmât, therefore सर्वौषधम् sarvauṣadham, the medicine (remedy) for all kinds of diseases ; mental or bodily or spiritual ; उच्यते uchyate, is said ; सर्वं sarvam, all ; वै vai, verily : एतत् êtat, this ; नामा nâmâ, name ; आप्नुवंति apnuvanti, become ; ये ye, those only ; अन्नम् annam, that god ब्रह्म brahma, that brahma in food (god in food) उपास्ते upaste, revere, worship ; अन्नं annam, food ; हि hi, because ; भूतानां bhûtanam of the created beings ; ज्येष्ठं jyeṣṭham, great ; तस्मात् tasmât, therefore ; सर्वौषिधं sarvausadham, panacea ; उच्यते uchyate, is said ; अन्नात् annât ; भूतानि bhutani, created beings ; जायंते jâyante, are produced. जातानि jâtâni , born ones ; अन्नेन annena, by means of food ; वर्धंते vardhante, grow ; अद्यते adyate, is eaten ; अत्ति atti, eats ; च cha, and ; भूतानि bhutani, beings.

5. There, this verse is appropriate. "From food certainly, the animal kingdom which is on the earth proceeds ; then they live on the food ; then unto it they return in the end. Because food is the source of the created beings, it is, therefore,

called the medicine of all. All those who worship food as Brahma, obtain all sorts of food ; because food is the source of the created beings, it is, therefore, called the medicine of all. From food the created beings are born ; the born ones are nourished by food ; it is eaten and the created beings eat it ; it is therefore, called food (anna).

Commentary,

The present verse has been bodily taken from elsewhere as said in the opening part of it ; it describes the excellence of food. All the animals whether oviparous or viviparous are produced from food, they are nourished by it and ultimately on death they return to it. The food which is no other than Aniruddha is the source of life and is the refuge of all afflicted persons (Ausadha). The fruit that accrues to a devotee who worships Aniruddha as Brahma is that he obtains Brahma. The verse concludes by repeating that food is the source of life and death and is, therefore, appropriately called medicine ; it is eaten and all the creatures eat it ; because it is eaten, it is called *anna* derived from *ad*, to eat.

तस्माद्वाएतस्मादन्नरसमयात् । अन्योंतरआत्माप्राणमयः । तेनैषपूर्णः । सवाएषपुरुषविधएव । तस्यपुरुषविधतां । अन्वयं पुरुषविधः । तस्यप्राणएवशिरः । व्यानोदक्षिणःपक्ष. । अपान उत्तरःपक्षः । आकाशआत्मा । पृथिवीपुच्छंप्रतिष्ठा ॥ ६ ॥

तस्माद् tasmâd, by that; by power of creating ; वा vâ ; एतस्मात् etasmât, by this, (by its being full of food) ; अन्नरसमयात् annarasamayât, by its being full of food ; अन्यः anyaḥ, other than that which is of food ; अन्तरः antaraḥ, internal, inside the food-god ; आत्मा âtmâ, नियामकः, the god controlling it ; प्राणमयः prâṇâmayaḥ, वायुविकारप्राणमयकोशस्थः, residing in the place of prâṇa-wind which is a particular form of wind ; तेन tena, by that, residing in the prâṇa ; एषः eṣaḥ, this, residing in food ; पूर्णः pûrṇaḥ, filled by ; सः saḥ, that in prâṇah ; वै vai certainly ; एषः eṣaḥ, this in food ; पुरुषविधः puruṣavidhaḥ, पुरुषाकारः, of the person-god ; एव eva, just ; तस्य tasya, of God in prâṇaḥ ; पुरुषविधताम् puruṣavidhatâm, the form of the person ; अनु anu, after ; अयं ayaṃ, this ; पुरुषविधः puruṣavidhaḥ, shape, this food-god has just the same form as the prâṇa god, as the former is formed just after the manner of the latter; तस्य tasya, of that of food; प्राण: prâṇaḥ, upbreathing; एव eva, (laying force on upbreathing); शिर: śiraḥ, head; व्यान: vyâ-naḥ, विशेषेण अनिति व्यानाख्य:, the wind circulating throughout the body; दक्षिण: dakṣiṇaḥ, right; पक्ष: pakṣaḥ, hand; अपान: apânaḥ, foul air; उत्तर: uttaraḥ, left; पक्ष: pakṣaḥ, wing; आकाश: âkâśaḥ ether; उदान:, the wind in the throat; आत्मा âtmâ, मध्यदेह: the central body, the authority there; पृथिवी, prithivî, earth; समान: the wind in the navel; पुच्छम्, puchchham, the trunk; प्रतिष्ठा pratiṣṭhâ, the feet.

6. Certainly from that, from this made of food there is another internal self made of vital air. It is full of it. It is certainly an imitation of the puruṣa only; this copy of the puruṣa is after the imitation of the puruṣa. His vital air is certainly head; the air that pervades the whole body is the southern wing; the filthy air is the northern wing; ether is soul; the earth is the tail which is the basis.

Commentary.

The verse proceeds to describe the second kośa called Prâṇa-maya; inside Aniruddha there is another deity called Pradyumna who is represented by the vital air. The envelope or case called Aniruddha is filled up entirely with Pradyumna who is here called Prâṇamaya kośa. Pradyumna pervading the case or head of vital air is in the form of Puruṣa; the other case made up of food and pervaded by Aniruddha is a copy thereof, The verse proceeds to describe the different parts. (Prâṇah, the vital air) is compared with the head, the vyâna (air that pervades the whole body) is compared with the right hand; the filthy air is compared with the left hand; ether and earth represent Samâna and Udâna, the winds pervading the umbilical region and throat. The middle part of Pradyumna's body called Udâna is compared with the tail; the Samâna is compared with the feet. According to Ânanda Tirtha Pradyumna is the Prâṇamaya Kośa.

तदप्येषश्लोकोभवति । प्राणंदेवाअनुप्राणं तिमनुष्याः पशवश्चये । प्राणोहिभूतानामायुः । तस्मात्सर्वायुषमुच्यते । सर्वमेवतआयुर्यंति । येप्राणं ब्रह्मोपासते । प्राणोहिभूताना मायुः । तस्मात्सर्वायुषमुच्यतइति । तस्यैषएवशारीर आत्मा । यःपूर्वस्य ॥ ७ ॥

तद् tad, on that; अपि api, also; एषः eṣaḥ, this; श्लोकः ślokaḥ ; भवति bhavati, becomes; देवाः मनुष्याः पशवः च ये प्राणं अनुप्राणन्ति; देवाः devâḥ, gods; मनुष्याः manuṣyâḥ, men; पशवः paśavaḥ, beasts and other lower animals; च cha, and ; ये ye, whoever they be, all of them; प्राणम् prâṇam, prâṇa; अनु anu, after ; प्राणन्ति prâṇanti, चेष्टते do their work. All those who do their work when they are animated by prâṇa, the god of breathing ; हि hi, because ; प्राणः prâṇah, the prana-god (is) ; भूतानाम् bhûtânâm, of beings ; आयुः âyuḥ, life, the chief support of life ; तस्मात् tasmât, therefore ; सर्वायुषम् sarvâyuṣam, (सर्वायुषः प्राणमयः) one which is the life of all, ये प्राणं ब्रह्म उपासते ते सर्वमायुरेव यंति ; ये ye, अधिकारिणः, (those who are able) ; प्राणं prâṇam, the prâṇa god ; ब्रह्म Brahma (to be brahma) ; उपासते upâsate, जानन्ति, know ; ते te, those persons ; सर्वमायुः sarvamâyuḥ, whole life ; मोक्षं mokṣam, salvation ; यंति yamti, सर्वं आयुर्यन्ति, obtaining salvation, प्राणोहि भूतानामायुः तस्मात्सर्वायुषं उच्यते (सर्वायुषः) ; इति iti, thus went the verse : तस्य tasya, of the food-god ; शारीरः आत्मा, śârîraḥ âtma, देहिरूपः आत्मा ; एषः eṣaḥ, this prâṇa-god. The meaning is that this prâṇa-god resides in the food-god as soul in a body ; यः yaḥ; the food-god ; पूर्वस्य pûrvasya of the former अन्नमयः (आत्मा).

7. There this verse is appropriate. The gods breathe after the vital air, the men and animals also. Because the vital air is the life of the created beings, it is therefore called whole life. Those who worship the vital air as Brahma, reach the whole length of life. Because the vital air is the life of the created beings, it is, therefore, called whole life. It is the embodied soul of this as of the former.

Commentary.

In connection with the Prâna Kośa, there is a verse the substance of which is that the gods, men and animals live by breathing ; breath is, therefore, life and is called so. The fruit that accrues to one who worships Pradyumna the presiding deity of the Prâṇa koṣa, is, that he attains longevity. The Prâṇamaya kośa represented by Pradyumna is the soul of the Annamaya kośa represented by Aniruddha.

तस्माद्वा एतस्मात्प्राणमयात् । अन्योंतरआत्मामनोमयः तेनैषपूर्णः । सवाएषपुरुषविधएव । तस्यपुरुषविधतां । अन्वयं-

पुरुषविधः । तस्ययजुरेवशिरः । ऋग्दक्षिणःपक्षः । सामोत्तरः पक्षः । आदेशआत्मा । अथर्वांगिरसःपुच्छंप्रतिष्ठा ॥ ८ ॥

तस्माद्वा एतस्मात् अन्यः tasmâdva etasmât anyah, different from that the food-god or the prâṇa-god ; अन्तरः आत्मा antaraḥ âtmâ ; internal self ; मनोमयः manomayaḥ, full of knowledge ; the knowledge-god; तेन tena, मनोमयेन आत्मना, by the knowledge-god, एषः eṣaḥ, this prâṇa-god; पूर्णः pûrṇaḥ, is occupied by, is filled by; सवा एषः savâ eṣaḥ, that knowledge-god or this prâṇa-god; पुरुषविधः puruṣavidhaḥ, has a body just of the shape of the person; तस्य पुरुषविधताम् अनु अयं पुरुषविधः tasya puruṣavidha tâm anu ayaṃ puruṣavidhaḥ, this prâṇa-god has a body just after the fashion of the body of the knowledge-god ; तस्य tasya, of the knowledge-god ; यजुः yajuḥ, yajurvedah; ऋक् साम ṛik sâma ; आदेशः â leśah, the doctrine is the âtma ; अथर्वांगिरसः atharvâṃgirasaḥ, the verses of the Atharva Veda (are the trunk and feet)

8. Certainly from that from this made of vital air, there is another internal self made of mind. It is full of it. It is certainly an imitation of the puruṣa ; this copy of the puruṣa is after the imitation of puruṣa only, Yaju is his head; Rig is southern wing; Sâma is the northern wing; the injunction is soul ; the Atharvângirasas is the tail which is the basis.

Commentary.

The verse describes the third kośa called manomaya kośa pervaded by Saṃkarṣaṇa. It is inside the prâṇamaya kośa which was described in the preceding verse. The prânamaya kośa presided over by Pradyumna is thoroughly filled up with the manomaya kośa presided over by Saṃkarṣana. Saṃkarṣana is the the shape of the Puruṣa ; the prâṇamaya kośa presided over by Pradyumna is after him The head of Saṃkarṣana is the Yajur Veda, the Rigveda is his right hand; the Sâma Veda is his left hand ; the Vedic injunction contained in the Brâhmaṇa is his middle part, The Riṣis known as Atharvangirasas are his feet or tail.

तदप्येषश्लोकोभवति । यतोवाचोनिवर्तंते । अप्राप्यमनसा-सह । आनंदंब्रह्मणोविद्वान् । नबिभेतिकदाचनेति । तस्यैषएवशारीरआत्मा । यःपूर्वस्य ॥ ९ ॥

यतः yataḥ. from which; वाचः vâchaḥ, words; मनसा सह manasâ saha, together with the mind; अप्राप्य aprâpya, not reaching (the bliss) निवर्तंते nivartamte, return; ब्रह्मणः brahmaṇaḥ, of Brahma; आनन्दं ânandam, bliss; विद्वान् vidvân, he who knows; न बिभेति navibheti, does not fear, gets salvation; कदाचन kadâchana, ever. He who knows the bliss of Brahman, whence (from which bliss) words together with the mind not being able to reach it (the bliss) return, does never fear (gets salvation); तस्य एषः शारीरः आत्मा tasya eṣah śârîrah âtmâ, this knowledge-god lives in the prâṇa-god as soul in a body; यः पूर्वस्य yaḥ pûrvasya, which prâṇa-god is of the former food-god.

9. There this verse is apropriate. One who knows Brahma full of bliss, whence speech with mind comes back without reaching, is never afraid. It is the embodied soul as of the previous.

Commentary.

The fruit that accrues to one who knows Brahma to be full of bliss which speech and mind can not describe and imagine, is that he becomes liberated from the world. This manomaya kośa pervaded by Saṃkarṣana is the soul of the Prâṇamaya presided over by Pradyumna, just as the latter is the soul of the annamaya kośa pervaded by Aniruddha.

तस्माद्वाएतस्मान्मनोमयात् । अन्योंतरआत्माविज्ञानमयः । तेनैषपूर्णः । सवाएषपुरुषविधएव । तस्यपुरुषविधतां । अन्वयंपुरुषविधः । तस्यश्रद्धैवशिरः । ऋतंदक्षिणःपक्षः । सत्यमुत्तरःपक्षः । योगआत्मा । महःपुच्छंप्रतिष्ठा ॥ १० ॥

तस्माद्वा एतस्माद् मनोमयात् tasmâtdvâ etasmâd manomayât, other than that prâṇa-god or this knowledge-god; अन्तरः आत्मा antaraḥ âtmâ, internal self. विज्ञानमयः vijñânamayaḥ, विशेषज्ञानप्राचुर्येण निमित्तेन विज्ञानमयः, of understanding; तेन एषः पूर्णः, tena eṣaḥ pûrṇaḥ, that vijñâna-god fills this mind-god; स वा एषः पुरुषविध एव sa vâ eṣaḥ puruṣavidhah eva, तस्य पुरुषविधतां अयं पुरुषविधः, the body of mind-god is in imitation of the vijñâna god; श्रद्धा śradhdâ, belief; ऋतं ritam, right knowledge; सत्यं satyam, true speeeh and action; योगः, yogaḥ, application; महः mahaḥ, the great,

10. Certainly from that, from this made of mind, there is another internal self made of intelligence; it is full of it. It is certainly an imitation of the Puruṣa only ; this copy of the puruṣa is after the imitation of the puruṣa. Faith is his head ; right (knowledge) is the southern wing ; truth is the northern wing: yoga is the soul. The great is the tail which is the basis.

Commentary.

The verse proceeds to describe the vijñanamaya kośa pervaded by Vâsudeva. The Manomaya kośa pervaded by Saṃkarṣana is entirely filled up with the vijnanamaya kośa presided over by Vâsudeva. The faith is his head ; the right knowledge is his right hand ; the truth is his left hand Yoga *i. e*, control of the mind's activities is his waist or the middle part of the body ; the great one is his tail or the feet.

तदप्येषश्लोकोभवति ॥ विज्ञानंयज्ञंतनुते । कर्माणितनुतेपिच । विज्ञानंदेवाःसर्वे । ब्रह्मज्येष्ठमुपासते । विज्ञानंब्रह्मचेद्वेद । तस्माच्चेन्नप्रमाद्यति । शरीरेपाप्मनोहित्वा । सर्वान्कामान्त्समश्नुतइति । तस्यैषएवशारीरआत्मा । यः पूर्वस्यः ॥ ११ ॥

तदप्येष श्लोको भवति tadapyeṣa śloko bhavati, on that there is the following verse ; विज्ञानं vijñânaṃ, the god in understanding ; यज्ञम् yajñam, sacrifice ; तनुते tanute, performs ; कर्माणि karmâṇi, religious and other duties ; तनुते tanute, performs ; अपि api, also ; च cha, and ; सर्वे देवाः, ब्रह्म ज्येष्ठविज्ञानमुपासते sarvedevâḥ brahmajyeṣthavijñânamupâsate; all gods worship the god of understanding as the oldest Brahman ; विज्ञानं ब्रह्म चेद् वेद vijñânaṃ brahmached veda, if one knows that the god of understanding is Brahma ; तस्माच्चेन्नप्रमाद्यति tasmâchennapramâdyati, and if he does not forget it (that it is so) ; शरीरे śarîre, existing in the body ; पाप्मनः pâpmanaḥ, evils ; हित्वा hitvâ, having left, giving up ; सर्वान् कामान् समश्नुते sarvân kâmân samaśnute, attains all desired objects ; इति iti, thus the verse ; तस्य एषः एव शारीरः आत्मा tasya eṣaḥ eva śarîraḥ âtmâ, this God in the understanding resides in the God of wind as the soul in a body ; यः पूर्वस्य yaḥ pûrvasya, which (the mind-god) is the soul of the former (the prâṇamaya-god).

11. There this verse is appropriate. Intelligence performs sacrifice, and also performs actions. All the gods worship intelligence as the supreme Brahma ; if one, therefore, does not neglect him, he by relinquishing all sins obtains all desires. It is the embodied soul of this as of the previous.

Commentary.

We have another quotation referred to in the present verse. Vâsudeva who pervades the Vijnânamaya kośa, being present amongst the priests and the sacrificers performs the sacrifice and its subordinate parts. If one realises Vâsudeva who pervades the Vijñânamaya kośa as Brahma, he has his desires accomplished. The rest is to be explained as was done in the preceding verses.

तस्माद्वाएतस्माद्विज्ञानमयात् । अन्योंतरआत्मानंदमयः । तेनैषपूर्णः । सवाएषपुरुषविधएव । तस्यपुरुषविधतां । अन्वयंपुरुषविधः । तस्यप्रियमेवशिरः । मोदोदक्षिणःपक्षः । प्रमोदउत्तरःपक्षः । आनंदआत्मा । ब्रह्मपुच्छंप्रतिष्ठा । तदप्येषश्लोकोभवति ॥ असन्नेवसभवति । असद्ब्रह्मेतिवेदचेत् । अस्तिब्रह्मेतिचेद्वेद । संतमेनंततोविदुरिति । तस्यैषएवशारीरआत्मा । यपूर्वस्य ॥ १२ ॥

तस्माद्वा एतस्माद् अन्यः tasmâd vâ etasmâd anyaḥ, different from the mind-god or this understanding god ; अन्तरः आत्मा आनन्दमय antaraḥ âtmâ ânandamayaḥ; there is one inside which is formed of bliss ; तेन एषः पूर्णः, tena eṣaḥ pûrṇaḥ, the bliss-god fills the whole of this understanding ; सः वा एषः पुरुषविधः एव saḥ vâ eṣaḥ puruṣavidhaḥ eva, that or this has got body ; तस्य पुरुषविधतामनु अयं पुरुषविधः tasya puruṣavidhatâm-anu ayaṃ puruṣavidhaḥ, the body of this (understanding-god) is exactly like that (the bliss-god) ; तस्य प्रियमेव शिरः tasya priyameva śiraḥ, pleasure is its head ; मोदः modaḥ, satisfaction ; प्रमोदः pramodaḥ, great satisfaction ; आनन्दः ânandaḥ, bliss ; ब्रह्म पुच्छं प्रतिष्ठा brahma puchchhaṃ pratiṣṭhâ, Brahma is its trunk and feet ; तदप्येषः श्लोकः भवति, ब्रह्म असद् इति वेद चेत् स असन्नेव भवति । असद् asad, not existing; if he knows that Brahma does not exist, he becomes unhappy ; असन्नेव दुःखीएव, unhappy ;

अस्ति ब्रह्म इति चेद् वेद asti brahma iti ched veda, if he knows that brahma does exist ; सन्तं santaṃ सुखिनं, मुक्तियेाग्यं Happy, worthy to get salvation ; एनं enaṃ, this ; विदुः viduḥ, they know, then they know him to be happy (worthy of salvation) ; तस्य एष; एव शारीरः आत्मा tasya eṣaḥ eva śârîraḥ âtmâ, this bliss-god is the soul of that god of understanding ; यः पूर्वस्य yaḥ pûrvasya, which (understanding-god) is that of the former (the mind god).

12. Certainly from that, from this full of intelligence, there is another internal self full of happiness. It is full of it. It is certainly an imitation of the puruṣa only : this copy of the puruṣa is after the imitation of the puruṣa. Pleasure is his head; joy is the southern wing ; satisfaction is the northern wing; happiness is the soul; Brahma is the tail which is the basis. There this verse is appropriate who thinks Brahma to be non-existent, but he himself becomes non-existent. If one believes Brahma to be existent they know him existent. It is the embodied soul of this as of the previous.

Commentary.

The verse describes the Ânandamaya kośa presided over by Nârâyaṇa. Pleasure is the wished for object of every one ; it is compared with the head of Nârâyaṇa. Joy arising from the worldly objects is compared with the right wing ; exessive joy is compared with the left wing. Happiness is the middle part of the body. Brahma is compared with the tail which is the basis of the whole human structure. The fruit that accrues to one who denies the existence of everything with the exception of the supreme and individual souls, is that he becomes unhappy but if one believes the supreme soul to be different from 'the individual soul' the people know him fit for salvation. The rest is to be explained as in the preceding verses.

अथातोनुप्रश्नाः । उताविद्वानमुं लोकंप्रेत्य । कश्चनग
च्छनी३ । आहोविद्वानमुं लोकंप्रेत्य । कश्चित्समश्नुता३उ ॥ १३

अथ atha, now ; अतः ataḥ, hence ; अनुप्रश्नाः anupraśnâh, ब्रह्मोकानुसारि वरुणेन ब्रह्मणं पृष्टाः प्रश्नाः अवसरप्राप्ताः पश्नाः, questions put to Brahmâ by Varuṇa when he found time to do so. There are three questions now. The first is उत अविद्वान् (अपियः) कश्चन प्रेत्य अमुं लोकं गच्छति । आहो विद्वान्-प्रेत्य अमुं

लोकं गच्छति । उत uta, or ; अविद्वान् avidvân, one who does not know ; कश्चन kaśchana, some-body ; pretya, after he dies ; अमुं लोकं amuṃ lokam, the heaven ; गच्छति gachchati, goes ; आहो âho, oh then ; विद्वान् vidvân, one who knows ; प्रेत्य अमुं लोकं गच्छति pretya amuṃ lokam gachchhati, goes to that world ; The full meaning is "Is it that a person ignorant of Brahma goes to heaven and if so, then is it not that the non-ignorant also goes to heaven ?". The second question is विद्वान् इति अत्र अपि किं सर्वः अपि गच्छति कश्चित् एव vidvân iti atra api kiṃ sarvaḥ api gachchhati kaśchit eva, In case a knower goes, is it that any body goes and thus all go ? The third question is सर्वे अपि इति अत्र अपि किं सर्वेऽपि सम्यक् (सम्) अश्नुते [प्राप्नोति gets] ब्रह्म । उत कश्चिदेव प्राप्नोति न सर्वे ; supposing all go to the other world is it that all get Brahma equally well ? or is it that someboby only gets it and all do not ?. उ U ; अभ्युपगम संक्षेप वाची अयम् उकारः this U is the word expressing affirmation for the last question, do all wise men attain ? do they attain it well ? The answer given by उ is कश्चिदेव ज्ञानी विरंचिपदयोग्यः समश्नुते अज्ञानी नैव ब्रह्म प्राप्नोति । ज्ञानिनोऽखिलाः प्राप्नुवंति Some wise man who is worthy of the place of Brahma gets it well. The ignorant does in no way get Brahma. All the wise men do get it. Whole of this answer is briefly denoted by उ (as Brahma was in contemplation he could not give more time for answering it).

13. Now as to the questions whether any ignorant person goes to the yonder world after departure or any knowing man after departure goes to the other world ?

Commentary.

Varuṇa puts three questions to Brahmâ. I. Does any person who does not know Brahma attain heaven ? Does only a person who knows Brahma attain heaven ? II. Do all persons knowing Brahma attain heaven or only some one of them ? III. Do some of the persons knowing Brahma attain heaven but not all ?

According to Sâyaṇâchârya, the verse contains four questions. I. Does an ignorant man go to heaven ? II Does he not ? III. Does a knowing person attain heaven ? if so an ignorant man who has everything in common with the knowing man attains heaven. IV. If an ignorant man does not attain heaven, does not the knowing man also attain it ?

सोकामयत । बहुःस्यांप्रजायेयेति । सतपोतप्यत । सतप स्तसवा । इदँ सर्वमसृजत । यदिदंकिंच । तत्सृष्टा । तदेवा

नुप्राविशत् । तदनुप्रविश्य । सच्चत्यच्चाभवत् । निरुक्तंचा निरुक्तंच । निलयनंचानिलयनंच । विज्ञानंचाविज्ञानंच । सत्यं चानृतंचसत्यमभवत् । यदिदंकिंच तत्सत्यमित्याचक्षते ॥१४॥

सः.........(अहं)प्रजायेय बहुःस्याम् इति अकामयत । सः saḥ, âtmâ ; प्रजायेय prajâyeya, जगत्सृजानि I shall create the world and the things in it ; बहुः bahuḥ, many ; स्याम् syâm, I shall be i. e. I shall manifest myself in many forms ; इति iti, refers to the above two sentences ; अकामयत akâmayata, desired ; सः saḥ; अतप्यत atapyata, practised penances; स तपस्तप्त्वा sa tapastaptvâ, he by practising penances (by the force of his penances) ; इदँ सर्वम्असृजत (asṛijata) स्वोदरस्थ जगद्बहिर्निर्यापयामास created, (brought forth this world which was formerly in him); यदिदंकिंच yadidam kiṃcha, whatever exists here; तत् tat (that); सृष्ट्वा sṛiṣtvâ, after creating all that; तत् tat, एव eva; अनुप्राविशत् anuprâviśat, entered the very thing he created; तत् tat; अनुप्रविश्य anupraviśya after entering that ; सच्च sat cha, सीदति अवसादयति इति सत् existence (so called God) what is manifest ; त्यत् tyat, च cha, नियामकः controlling or governing, what is not manifest (so called-god) ; निरुक्तं niruktaṃ, defined ; that about which one may speak. अनिरुक्तं aniruktaṃ, that about which one can not speak, undefined ; निलयनं nilayanaṃ, support; अनिलयनं anilayanam, not a support ; विज्ञानं vijñânaṃ, knowledge ; अविज्ञानं avijñânaṃ, want of knowledge ; सत्यं satyaṃ, truth ; अनृतं anṛitaṃ, false-hood ; सत्यं प्राणरूपं जगत् the animate world ; here त्यत् denotes अनिरुक्तं, निलयनं, विज्ञानं and सत् denotes निरुक्त, अनिलयन, अविज्ञान. यदिदं किंच all this ; तत् tat, that (which was impermanent before) ; सत्यं satyaṃ, pure ; आचक्षते âchakaṣate, call (that pure) ;

14. He desired, let me be many, let me be born; He performed a penance; after performing a penance, he created all this whatever it is. After creating it, he entered into it; having entered into it, he became manifest and non-manifest, defined and non-defined, support and non-support, knowledge and ignorance, truth and falsehood. Truth became all this which exists; they, therefore, call it truth.

Commentary.

The verse embodies the reply. The Supreme soul in order to create the universe by assuming manifold forms, desired *i e.,* a desire for the creation arose ; accordingly he performed a penance or meditated. After meditation, he created or evolved out from his belly every thing which is in the universe. After creating it he entered into it ; after it he became manifest and non-manifest ; he became defined by granting bounty and undefined by reason of having no end and being beyond description. He is a support by reason of supporting the universe but non-support by imparting wickedness to it. He is knowledge by being omniscient ; by imparting ignorance, the world pervaded by him is ignorant. He is truth by imparting good to the universe but by making it fragile and weak, it (universe) is false. The word 'Sattya' (truth) is made up of *Sat+tya.* Brahma is *tya* because he is undefined, support and knowledge. Satya or truth is the universe represented by the goddess of fortune and life. *Sat* is defined non-support, ignorance and falsehood ; it is some universe other than matter, life and *Mahat*. He is therefore known as truth (Satya) by reason of being pure and sinless ; the elders accordingly call the universe pervaded by him by the name of truth.

तदप्येषश्लोकोभवति । असद्वाइदमग्रआसीत् । ततोवैसदजायत । तदात्मानँस्वयमकुरुत । तस्मात्तत्सुकृतमुच्यतइति । यद्वैतत्सुकृतंरसोवैसः । रसँह्येवायंलब्ध्वानंदीभवति । कोह्येवान्यात्कःप्राण्यात् । यदेषआकाशआनंदोनस्यात् । एषह्येवानंदयाति ॥ १५ ॥

इदम् idam, this ; अग्रे agre, formerly before ; असत् asat, (being) devoid of form not existing. Such was God असन्नामा नारायणः मूलरूपी आसीत् । ततः tataḥ, from that formless god ; सत् sat, having a form and so existing ; सन्नामा वासुदेवः अजायत ajâyat, was produced ; तत् स वासुदेवाख्यरूप, that form, आत्मानं âtmânaṃ, itself (self-god) ; स्वयं swayaṃ, in person ; अकुरुत akuruta, made, formed ; तस्मात् tasmât, owing to his quality of manifesting himself in different forms ; तत् tat ; सुकृतं sukṛitam, well formed; उच्यते uchyate, is called ; इति iti, thus the verse ; यद् yad, which ; एतत् etat, this ; सुकृतं sukṛitaṃ, वासुदेवः God with forms ; सः saḥ, he ; रसः rasaḥ, आनन्द मयः, formed of bliss ; हि hi, because ; अयं, ayaṃ, this wise man, (ज्ञानी) ; रसं एव rasam eva, आनंदरूपं एव eva, only the god formed of bliss ; लब्ध्वा labdhvâ, after getting ; आनंदीभवति

anamdî bhavati, becomes cheerful; यद् yad, if; एष eṣa, this; आकाशः âkâśaḥ, the god called âkâśa; आनन्दः ânandaḥ, सुखस्वरूपः of the form of bliss; नस्यात् nasyât, not; कः हि एव अन्यात् kaḥ hi eva anyât who would then have breathed? कः प्राण्यात् kaḥ prâṇyât, who would have been animated to do work (नकोऽपि) na kaḥ api, none; एष एव eṣaḥ एव, this alone; आनंदयाति ânamdayâti, आनंदयति ânamdayti, makes (everything) blessed.

15. Here this verse is appropriate; there was non-entity in the beginning, thence came out entity. It made itself; it is therefore called self-made. That which is self-made is happiness; for one on obtaining happiness becomes happy. If this ether were not happiness, who can certainly act, who can breathe? Certainly this alone makes happy.

Commentary.

In the beginning before the creation there was Nârâyaṇa who is called 'non-entity' in the verse; from him proceeded Vâsudeva who is called entity here. Vâsudeva made himself into two; viz, Saṃkarṣaṇa and Pradyumna. Because he made himself into Saṃkarṣaṇa and Pradyumna, Vâsudeva, is called 'self-born' or well-done'. Vâsudeva who is self-born is happiness to those who are desirous of salvation; hence one on obtaining spiritual knowledge becomes happy. The verse assigns a reason in support of the view embodied herein; if the Lord who is here represented by ether were not happiness, the whole universe will be destroyed; for who can act or breathe? As he makes every one happy, he is, therefore, happiness personified.

यदाह्येवैषएतस्मिन्नदृश्येऽनात्म्येऽनिरुक्तेऽनिलयने ऽभयंप्रतिष्ठांविंदते । अथसोऽभयंगतोभवति ॥ यदाह्येवैषएतस्मिन्नुदरमंतरंकुरुते । अथतस्यभयंभवति । तत्वेवभयंविदुषोमन्वानस्य । तदप्येषश्लोकोभवति ॥ भीषास्माद्वातःपवते । भीषोदेतिसूर्यः । भीषास्मादग्निश्चेंद्रश्च । मृत्युर्धावतिपंचमइति ॥ १६ ॥

यदा yadâ, when; हि hi, because; एव eva, only ; एष ; esaḥ, this wise man (मुमुक्षु) एतस्मिन् etasmin, in this (god) ; अदृश्ये adriśye, in invisible ; अनात्म्ये anâtmye, जीवगुणहीने. in one which is without the qualities of a jîva. अनिरुक्ते anirukte, साकल्येननिर्वचनागोचरे undefined, not known only by a well arranged collection of words ; अनिलयने anilayane, not existing any where else.; अभयं (यथाभवति) abhayaṃ (yathâ bhavati) fearlessly ; प्रतिष्ठां pratisṭhâṃ, ध्यानरूपां प्रतिष्ठां a position of meditation, अथ, atha, then ; सः saḥ, the worshipper ; अभयं abhayaṃ, god ; गतःभवति gataḥ bhavati, reaches, obtains. The meaning is that he attains God not only by knowing his nature but by fearlessly contemplating over his qualities. He must know him theoretically and practically. यदा हि एव yadâ hi eva, एषः esaḥ, ज्ञानी, अज्ञः वा ajñaḥ vâ, the wise or the ignorant ; एतस्मिन् etasmin, in this god (Visṇu) ; उदरं udaraṃ उद a jiva, उदरं of the jivas (amongst themselves) ; अंतरं aṃtaraṃ, difference ; कुरुते kurute, मन्यते thinks, makes : भगवद्रूपाणां अन्योन्यं मूलरूपस्य च भेदं जानीते he (wise or unwise) who knows that the forms of God are different from each other and each of them different from the original ; अथ तस्य भयं भवति atha tasya bhayaṃ bhavati, now he has to fear ; तत् तु एव भयं विदुषः अमन्वानस्य tat tu eva bhayaṃ viduṣaḥ amanvânasya, but that thinking that there is difference, there is fear to a wise as well as to an unwise person; अमन्वानस्य Amanvânasya, to an unwise ; the wise has some fear before he gets salvation, afterwards he is without fear. While the unwise has fear from this world, and the worldly life. अस्माद् asmâd, अस्य ब्रह्मणः भयेन, through the fear of Brahma ; भीषा bhîṣâ, through fear ; वातः vâtaḥ, wind, पवते pavate, blows ; उदेति udeti , rises ; सूर्यः sûryaḥ, the sun ; अग्निः agniḥ, fire पाचयति pâchayati, (heats) digests, cooks ; इन्द्रः Indraḥ, the Lord of the gods (protects the being and gives rain) ; पंचमः मृत्युः paṃchamaḥ mrityuḥ, the fifth god of death, यमः धावति dhâvati, goes to destroy and thus to do his duty through the fear of Brahma.

16. When one certainly obtains fearlessness as refuge in this invisible, incorporeal, undefined, and in the independent, he then becomes fearless; when one makes even a little difference in him, then there is fear for him, for fear arises to the wise and ignorant. There this verse is appropriate; wind blows out of fear arising from him, from fear the sun rises, from this fear fire, Indra and the fifth death (god) discharge their respective functions.

Commentary.

When a devotee makes Hari, the mark or object of his meditation and considers him perceptible by spiritual knowledge, devoid of the qualities of the corporate soul and independent, he becomes fearless or united with him; but if, on the other hand, one makes a slight distinction amongst the different manifestations of Viṣṇu there is fear of death for such a person. There is fear for both, the wise and ignorant; to the former there is slight fear so long he is not liberated; subsequently he becomes fearless and to the ignorant there is always fear from trans migration. In support of this view there is a quotation in the verse that owing to the fear of Brahma, every deity discharges his duty; as for instance wind blows, the sun rises, the fire burns, Indra rains and death discharges its duty. Sâyaṇa has interpreted 'for fear arises to the wise and ignorant' in the text as meaning that the fear of death arises to the wise man if he is ignorant of the spiritual science.

सैषानंदस्यमीमाँसाभवति । युवास्यात्साधुयुवाध्यायकः । आशिष्टोदृढिष्ठोबलिष्ठोबलिष्ठः । तस्येयंपृथिवीसर्वावित्तस्य पूर्णास्यात् । सएकोमानुषआनंदः । तेयेशतंमानुषाआनंदाः । सएकोमनुष्यगंधर्वाणामानंदः ॥ १७ ॥

सा एषा sâ esâ, that this ; आनन्दस्य ânandasya, of bliss ; मीमाँसा mîmâṃsâ, examination ; भवति bhavati, is, forms, becomes ; युवा yuvâ, विष्णुना सह गन्ता, तरुणः वा, one who accompanies God, or a young man ; स्यात् syât, should be ; साधु sâdhu, साधुभिर्गुणै युक्तः of good qualities ; साधु युवा sâdhu yuvâ, one accompanying God, विष्णुनायुतः । अध्यायकः âdhyâyakaḥ, सम्यगध्ययनकर्ता ; a good student ; आशिष्ठः âśiṣthaḥ, नित्यपूर्णसुखवान् always entirely happy ; दृढिष्ठः, dṛiḍhiṣthaḥ, very firm and resolute in mind ; बलिष्ठः baliṣthaḥ, very strong ; all the above, mean that he should be a free man ; तस्य tasya, of that person who is so free ; पृथिवी prithvî, land ; सर्वा sarvâ, all (his land) ; वित्तस्य पूर्णा वित्तेन पूर्णा (be) rich in (natural wealth) ; सः saḥ, the bliss (the person obtains in that prosperous state of his) एकः ekaḥ, the only one (of its kind) ; मानुष्यः, mânuṣyaḥ, of a man (who is thus free) ; ते te, those kinds of happiness ; ये शतं ye śatam, which (taken) a hundred times ; मानुष्यः mânuṣyaḥ, human ; आनंदाः

anaṁdâḥ, happiness ; सः saḥ, that (which is formed of hundred units of human happiness) ; एकः ekaḥ, one ; मनुष्यगन्धर्वाणाम् manuṣya gandharvâṇâm, of men and Gandharvas who are free; आनन्दः ânandaḥ, joy.

17. It is this that is fit for the determination of happiness. Let there be a young man, a young man of good qualities well-read, full of pleasure, most firm and most powerful ; let there be this earth full of wealth for him. This is one unit of human happiness. Such hundred numbers of human happiness make one happiness of human Gandharvas.

Commentary.

Now the verse proceeds to explain what happiness or bliss is ; it is explained by giving an idea of what it can be. It takes up a hypothetical case ; let there be a young man of good qualities, learned, full of all worldly pleasures, firm and strong ; let there be a world full of wealth for him. Consider what happiness he has. This is one unit of human happiness. Such hnndred units of human happiness constitute one unit of happiness of human Gandharvas.

श्रोत्रियस्यचाकामहतस्य । तेयेशतंमनुष्यगंधर्वाणामानंदाः । सएकोदेवगंधर्वाणामानंदः । श्रोत्रियस्यचाकामहतस्य । तेयेशतंदेवगंधर्वाणामानंदाः । सएकःपितॄणांचिरलोकलोकानामानंदः । श्रोत्रियस्यचाकामहतस्य । तेयेशतंपितॄणांचिरलोकलोकानामानंदाः । सएकआजानजानांदेवानामानंदाः । श्रोत्रियस्यचाकामहतस्य । तेयेशतमाजानजानांदेवानामनंदाः । सएकःकर्मदेवानांदेवानामानंदः ॥ १८ ॥

श्रोत्रियस्य Śrotṛiyasya, of a Brâhmin who has learnt the Vedas ; अकामहतस्य च akâmahatasya cha, and of one who is not affected by desires, so the human bliss taken hundred times is the unit bliss of man-gandharvas and of a Vedic Brâhmin ; ते ये शतं मनुष्यगंधर्वाणां आनन्दाः

hundred times the bliss of the man-gandharvas, स एको देवगन्धर्वाणां आनन्दः, that is the unit of bliss of the God-Gandharvas, श्रोत्रियस्य च अकामहतस्य, also it is a unit of bliss of the Vedic Brâhman ; ते ये शतं देवगन्धर्वाणां आनन्दाः, Hundred times the bliss of the God Gandharvas, स एकः पितृणां चिरलोकलोकानां आनन्दः, श्रोत्रियस्य च अकामहतस्य that is the unit of the bliss of the Pitṛis who are the people of the fixed world ; it is the bliss of the Śrotriya who is not affected by desires, ते ये शतं पितृणां चिरलोकलोकानां आनंदाः, Hundred times the bliss of the Pitri ; स एक अजानजानां देवानां आनन्दः, that is the unit of bliss of the unknown Gods and their issue ; श्रोत्रियस्य च अकामहतस्य, also of the Śrotriya who is not affected by desires ; ते ये शतं अजानजानां देवानांआनन्दाः स एकः कर्मदेवानां देवानां आनन्दः, Hundred times the bliss of the unknown Gods is the unit of the bliss of the Gods who have become Gods by means of their good actions ; आजानजानां âjânajânâṃ, देवेषु अकथिताः याः देवताः देवेषुअनाख्याताः ते आजानदेवाः तेषाम्, of those Gods whose names are not given in the list of Gods.

18. It is of one well-versed in the Vedas and without desires. Such hundred numbers of human gandharva's happiness make one unit of happiness of the divine gandharvas. It is of one well-versed in the Vedas and without desires. Such hundred numbers of the divine gandharva's happiness make one happiness of the manes who reside in permanent regions. It is of one well-versed in the Vedas and without desires. Such hundred numbers of happinessof the manes who reside in the permanent regions make one unit of happiness of those born in the family of the gods. It is one well versed in the Vedas and without desires. Such hundred numbers of happiness of those born in the family of the gods constitute one unit of happiness of those gods who attain heaven by action.

Commentary.

The verse goes on giving an idea of different standards of happiness or bliss. What is called human gandharva's happiness in the preceding verse is also the same happiness which arises to one who has studied the Vedas for their own sake without any worldly object in view. Such hundred units of the Gandharva's happiness make one unit of happiness of the divine Gandharvas. It also arises to a student of the Vedas. Hundred times greater is the bliss of the *manes* residing in the permanent regions ; hundred times greater is the standard of happiness of those who are born in the family of the gods ; still hundred times greater is the bliss of those who attain heaven by performing the Vedic sacrifice. All these different standards of happiness are enjoyed by a person who studies the Vedas for their own sake without any worldly object in view.

येकर्मणादेवानपियंति । श्रोत्रियस्यचाकामहतस्य । तेयेशतं कर्मदेवानांदेवानामानंदाः । सएकोदेवानामानंदः । श्रोत्रियस्यचाकामहतस्य । तेयेशतंदेवनामानंदाः । सएकइंद्रस्यानंदः । श्रोत्रियस्य चाकामहतस्य । तेयेशतमिंद्रस्यानंदाः । सएकोबृहस्पतेरानंदः । श्रोत्रियस्यचाकामहतस्य । तेयेशतंबृहस्पतेरानंदाः ॥१६॥

कर्मदेवाः karmadevâḥ, कर्मणां मध्ये देवत्वं प्राप्नुवन्ति ते कर्मदेवाः, those who become gods owing to their (good) actions ; ये ye, those who ; कर्मणा karmaṇâ ; कर्मणा मध्ये, in course of their actions ; देवान् devân, देवत्वं, the qualities of gods ; अपि यन्ति apiyanti, प्राप्नुवन्ति, obtain ; श्रोत्रियस्य च अकामहतस्य also of the Vedic Brahmin who is not affected by desires ; ते ये शतं कर्मदेवानां देवानां आनन्दाः । स एको देवानां आनन्दाः श्रोत्रियस्य च अकामहतस्य । hundred times the bliss of the deed-God makes one unit of bliss of the (real) Gods also of the Vedic Brahmana who is not affected by desires ; ते ये शतं देवानामानन्दाः । स एकः इन्द्रस्य आनन्दः । श्रोत्रियस्य च अकामहतस्य । Hundred times the bliss of the gods is equal to the unit of bliss of Indra also that of a śrotriya not affected by desires; ते ये शतं इन्द्रस्यआनन्दाः । स एको बृहस्पतेः आनन्दः । श्रोत्रियस्य च अकामहतस्य । hundered times the bliss of Indra make the unit of bliss of Brihaspati also, that of the śrotriya who is without desires ; ते ये शतं बृहस्पतेरानन्दा.

19. Who becomes a god by actions. It is of one well-versed in the Vedas and without desires. Such hundred numbers of happiness of the gods who attain heaven by action, make one unit of happiness of the gods. It is one well-versed in the Vedas without desires. Such hundred numbers of the god's happiness make one unit of happiness of

Indra. It is of one well versed in the Vedas without desires. Such hundred numbers of Indra's happiness make one unit of happiness of Brihaspati. It is of one well versed in the Vedas without desires. Such are hundred numbers of Brihaspati's happiness.

Commentary.

The verse is a continuation of the preceding verse and defines the gods who attained heavens by performing the sacrifical rites. They are not born gods but reach the position of the gods by performance of the vedic rites. Hundred times is the standard of happiness of the gods ; still hundred times greater is the standard of happiness of Indra ; still hundred times greater is the standard of happiness of Brihaspati ; all these different standards of happiness are enjoyed by a person who studies the Vedas for their own sake without any wordly object in view.

सएकःप्रजापतेरानंदः । श्रोत्रियस्यचाकामहतस्य । तेयेशतं प्रजापतेरानंदाः । सएकोब्रह्मणआनन्दःश्रोत्रियस्यचाकामहतस्य ॥ २० ॥

Hundred units of Brihaspati's bliss ; स एकः प्रजापतेरानन्दः । श्रोत्रियस्य च आकामहतस्य : make the unit of bliss of Prajâpati (Rudra is called so) also of a śrotriya devoid of desires ; ते ये शतं प्रजापते आनन्दाः । स एकः ब्रह्मणः आनन्दः । श्रोत्रियस्य च अकामहतस्य । Hundred times the Prajapati's bliss equal the unit of bliss of Brahma, also of the Śrotriya who is not struck by desires.

20. Make one happiness of Prajapati. It is also of one well-versed in the Vedas and without desires. Such hundred numbers of Prajâpati's happiness make one unit of happiness of Brahma. It is of one well-versed in the Vedas and without desires.

Commentary

The verse is connected with the proceding verse ; I have given the verses according to the reading of the Mâdhva school. Still hundred times greater is the standard of happiness of Rudra or Prajâpati; there is still hundred times greater happiness of Brahma : all these different standards of happiness are enjoyed by a person who studies the Vedas for their own sake without any worldly object in view.

सयश्चायंपुरुषे । यश्चासावादित्ये । सएकः । सयएवंवित् । अस्माल्लोकात्प्रेत्य । एतमन्नमयमात्मानमुपसंक्रामति । एतंप्राणमयमात्मानमुपसंक्रामति । एतंमनोमयमात्मानमुपसंक्रामति । एतंविज्ञानमयमात्मानमुपसंक्रामति । एतंमानन्दमयमात्मानमुपसंक्रामति ॥ २१ ॥

यः च अयं पुरुषे । यः च असौ आदित्येस एकः । यः yaḥ, who, अयं this; पुरुषे puruṣe, सर्वजीवसङ्घे, in all the human and animal bodies: यः yaḥ, who; असौ asau, that: आदित्ये âditye, in the sun; सः, saḥ, एकः ekaḥ, one and the same (Brahma); यः yaḥ, अधिकारी authorised, occupying a certain stage; एवंवित् evaṃvit, एवं जानन्, knows this fact; सः saḥ, he, अस्माल्लोकात्, asmâlokât, भौतिकदेहात्, from this physical body; प्रेत्य pretya देहं त्यक्तवा निर्गत्य departing after leaving this body; एतम् etam, this; अन्नमयम् आत्मानम्, annamayam âtmânam, the food-god or soul; उपसंक्रामति upasaṃ krâmati, goes to, attains; एतं प्राणमयमात्मनमुपसंक्रामति he reaches this breath god; एतं मनोमयमात्मानं उपसंक्रामति, he approaches this mind god; एतं विज्ञानमयमात्मानमुपसंक्रामति he approaches the understanding-god; एतं आनन्दमयमात्मानं उपसंक्रामति। he attains this soul formed of bliss.

21. He who is in the man and he who is in the sun are one (and the same) he who understands it after departure from this world becomes this self made of food, becomes this self made of vital air, becomes the self made of mind, becomes the self made of intelligence, becomes the self made of happiness.

Commentary.

Having given the questions and answers in the preceding verses the present verse shows the identity of the self in the man and the sun. The result that accrues to a devotee who understands this gradation becomes Aniruddha, Pradyumna, Sankarṣana and Vâsudeva.

तदप्येषश्लोकोभवति ॥ यतोवाचोनिवर्तंते । अप्राप्यमनसा सह । आनदब्रह्मणोविद्वान् । नविभेतिकुतश्चनेति। एतँहवाव

नतपति । किमहँसाधुनाकरवम् । किमहपापमकरवमिति । सयएवंविद्वानेतेआत्मानँस्पृणुते। उभेह्येवैषएतेआत्मानँस्पृणुते । यएवंवेद । इत्युपनिषत् ॥ ॐ ॥ सहनाववतु । सहनौभुनक्तु । सहवीर्यंकरवावहै । तेजस्विनावधीतमस्तुमा विद्विषावहै ॥ ओ३म् शांतिःशांतिःशांतिः ॥ २२ ॥

तदप्येष: श्लोकोभवति । on that there is this verse ; a person knowing that perfect bliss only obtains salvation ; यतो वाचो निवर्तन्ते । अप्राप्य मनसा सह । आनन्दं ब्रह्मणो विद्वान् । न बिभेति कुतश्चन ; He, who knows the bliss of the Brahman, whence words together with the mind, being unable to reach it, return, does not fear any body or thing. (becomes free, gets salvation) ; इति iti, thus the verse is complete ; एतं etaṃ, ज्ञानिनं this wise men (for whom there is no fear, who is free) ; ह ha, surely ; वाव न vâva na, नैव not even ; तपति कर्म tapati karma, troubles (the fruit of past action) ; अहं ahaṃ, I ; किम् kim, what ; साधु sâdhu, puṇyaṃ, good action ; नाकरवम् nâkaravam, did not do ; (by way of repentance) ; किम्, अहं, पापं evil अकरवम्, did I do ? thus he repents and so he is free from the fruits of good and bad deeds : स य एवं विद्वान् sa ya evaṃ vidvân, he who knows thus (in a free state) the Paramâtman ; एते ete, these ; पुण्यपापे good and bad actions ; स्पृणुते spriṇute, जहाति gives up (to friends and foes) ; to friends he gives good actions, to foes bad ones ; उभे ubhe, both ; हि hi because ; एव eva, also ; एते ete, these, (both) good and bad actions ; स्पृणुते spriṇute, gives up ; यः आत्मानं एव वेद yaḥ âtmânaṃ eva veda, he who knows Brahma to be one and to be formed of bliss ; इति उपनिषत् iti upaniṣat, (concludes) that this is secret (of the Vedas) ; then the शान्तिः —

22. There this verse is appropriate ; one who knows Brahma full of bliss whence speech with mind comes back without reaching it, is never afraid. It does not certainly make him repent. "Have I not done good ? Have I committed sin?" They leave the soul of one who understands this. They both certainly leave the soul of one who understands this. This is the secret. Om ! Let him protect us (both) together ; let him nourish us (both) together ; let us both show strength ,

let our learning be splendid ; let us (both) be not hostile (to each other.) Om., peace, peace, peace.

Commentary

The verse is the concluding part of the 2nd Vâlli ; it describes Brahma who is not an object of speech cr mind. You can not describe him or conceive him. A devotee who realises Brahma, is not afraid of death and does not repent at the time of death by thinking that he did not perform righteous acts or that he committed sin. He becomes perfectly liberated. Sin and virtue both leave him who understands it. No action, the fruit of which he has to reap, remains The verse concludes with the usual prayer of peace as read in the beginning of this Valli.

End of Brahma Valli.

Valli III Called Bhrigu Valli

ओंसहनाववतु । सहनौभुनक्तु । सहवीर्यं करवावहै । तेजस्विनावधीत मस्तुमाविद्विषावहै । ओं शान्तिः शान्तिः । शान्तिः । ओम् भृगुर्वैवारुणिः वरुणंपितरमुपससार । अधीहिभगवोब्रह्मेतितस्माएतत्प्रोवाच । अन्नंप्राणंचक्षुःश्रोत्रंमनोवाचमिति । तँहोवाच । यतोवाइमानिभूतानि जायंते । येनजातानिजीवंति । यत्प्रयंत्यभिसंविशंति । तद्विजिज्ञासस्व । तद्ब्रह्मेति ॥ १ ॥

The Śânti ; ओं सह नाववतु । मा विद्विषावहै ओं शान्तिः शान्तिः शान्तिः ॥ वारुणिः भृगुर्वै पितरं वरुणं उपससार। वारुणिः vâruṇiḥ, the son of Varuṇa ; भृगुः bhṛiguḥ, a sage named so ; वै vai, it is a known fact ; पितरं pitaraṃ, father ; उपससार upasasâra, went to (his father) ; अधीहि adhîhi, अध्यापय teach (me) ; भगवः bhagavaḥ, भगवन् O ! Lord ; ब्रह्म brahma ; इति iti, thus (saying this) ; तस्मा tasmâ, तस्मै to him, to Bhrigu ; एतत् etat, thiṣ, the following ; प्रोवाच provâcha, said ; अन्नं annaṃ, अन्नमयं अन्नं formed of food ; प्राणं prâṇaṃ, of breath ; चक्षुः chakṣuḥ, of eyes (the soul having the power of seeing all) ; मनः manaḥ', mind-god ; वाचम् vâcham, the speech-god ; तं हो वाच taṃ ho vâcha, he described him thus ; यतः yataḥ, from which Brahma ; इमानि imâni, these ; भूतानि

bhûtâni, beings ; जायन्ते jâyante, are born ; येन yena, by whose help, owing to whom ; जातानि jâtâni, born ones ; जीवन्ति jîvanti, live ; यत् yat, which (brahma) प्रयन्ति prayanti, go ; प्रलये pralaye, at the time of the general destruction ; संविशन्ति saṃvisanti, enter ; तद् tad, that ; तद्विषयकश्र- वणमननिदिध्यासनरूपा विजिज्ञासस्व vijijñâsasva, जिज्ञासां कुरु study, know well ; तद् tad, that ; ब्रह्म brahma, (know it).

I. Om ; let him protect us (both) together ; let him nourish us (both) together ; let us (both) show strength ; let our learning be splendid ; let us (both) be not hostile (to each other.) Om ! peace, peace, peace. Om ! Brigu, son of Varuṇa verily went to his father Varuṇa 'O ! master teach me Brahma.' He said to him "food, vital air, eye, ear, mind and speech" He told him, know him from whom, these created beings are born, by whom the beings live and into whom they merge ; he is Brahma.

Commentary.

The chapter opens with the usual prayer with which the last Valli commenced and ended. Bhṛigu went to his father and asked him to initiate him into Brahma Vidyâ or spiritual science. He told him all the koṣaṣ, viz, the Annamaya Prâṇamaya Manomaya, Vijnânamaya and Ânandmaya described in the preceding chapter ; then gave a definition of Brahma and directed him to enquire about him from whom the whole creation proceeds, by whom it is maintained and in whom it ultimately merges.

सतपोतप्यत । सतपस्तप्त्वा ॥ अन्नं ब्रह्मेतिव्यजा
नात् । अन्नाध्येवखल्विमानिभूतानिजाययंते । अन्नेनजाता
निजीवंति । अन्नंप्रयंत्यभिसंविशंतीति । तद्विज्ञाय ॥ २ ॥
पुनरेववरुणांपित्तरमुपससार । अधीहिभगवोब्रह्मेति ।
तं होवाच । तपसाब्रह्मविजिज्ञासस्व ॥

स तपः अतप्यत saḥ tapaḥ atapyata, he (Bhṛigu) meditated, thought over ; स तपस्तप्त्वा saḥ tapaḥ taptvâ, after meditating ; सः saḥ he ; अन्नं annaṃ, food and the god in it formed of it ; ब्रह्म इति brahma iti, to be Brahma ; व्यजानात् vyajânât, साक्षात्कृतवान् actually knew it to be so (food &c) ; अन्नात् annât, from food ; हि hi, because ; एव eva, only ; खलु khalu, verily ; इमानि imâni, these (which we see) ; भूतानि bhûtâni, beings ; जायन्ते jâyante, are produced ; अन्नेन annena, by the force or help of food ; जातानि jâtâni, the born ones ; जीवन्ति jîvanti, (are able to) live ; अन्नं प्रयन्ति अभिसंविशन्ति इति, the beings after death enter food ; तद्विज्ञाय tadvijñâya, experiencing that ; पुनरेव punareva, again ; वरुणं, पितरं varuṇam pitaram, his father Varuṇa ; उपससार upasasâra, approached ; अधीहि भगवो ब्रह्म इति, saying, lord teach us Brahma (further) ; तं हो वाच तम् ho vâcha, him (to Brighu) Varuna said ; तपसा ब्रह्म विजिज्ञासस्व, know Brahma actually by means of meditation, worship,and practice ; प्राणमयाख्यं ब्रह्मसाक्षात्कतुं अनुज्ञां देहि, or permit me to learn and to see through practice that it is formed of *breath*

2. He performed a penance ; after performing a penance, he came to know food to be Brahma, because from food are born all these created beings, by food the beings live and into food they ultimately merge. Knowing this he again went to Varuṇa, his father "well master, teach me Brahma" He said to him " enquire Brahma by means of penance."

Commentary

On this Bhrigu began to meditate; after meditation he came to the conclusion that presiding deity of the food was Brahma because Aniruddha fulfilled the requisites of the definition of Brahma given by his father. He thereupon went to him and again asked him to teach Brahma vidyâ ; he told him to make a further enquiry by means of meditation.

तपोब्रह्मेति । सतपोतप्यतसतपस्तप्त्वा: प्राणोब्रह्मेति व्याजानात् । प्राणाद्ध्येवखल्विमानिभूतानिजायंते । प्राणेन जातानिजीवंति । प्राणंप्रयंत्यभिसंविशंतीति । तद्विज्ञाय । पुनरेववरुणंपितरमुपससार । अधीहिभगवोब्रह्मेति । तंहोवाच तपसाब्रह्मविजिज्ञासस्व । तपोब्रह्मेति । सतपोतप्यत ।

सतपस्तप्त्वा ॥ मनोब्रह्मेतिव्यजानात् । मनसोह्येवखल्विमानिभूतानिजायंते । मनसाजातानिजीवंति । मनःप्रयंत्यभिसंविशंतीति । तद्विज्ञाय । पुनरेववरुणंपितरमुपससार । अधीहिभगवोब्रह्मेति । तंहोवाच । तपसाब्रह्मविजिज्ञासस्व । तपोब्रह्मेति । सतपोतप्यत । सतपस्तप्त्वा ॥ विज्ञानंब्रह्मेतिव्यजानात् । विज्ञानाद्ध्येयवखल्विमानिभूतानिजायंते । विज्ञानेनजातानिजीवंति । विज्ञानंप्रयंत्यभिसंविशंतीति । तद्विज्ञाय । पुनरेववरुणंपितरमुपससार । अधीहिभगवोब्रह्मेति । तंहोवाच । तपसाब्रह्मविजिज्ञासस्व । तपोब्रह्मेति । सतपोतप्यत । सतपस्तप्त्वा । आनंदोब्रह्मेतिव्यजानात् । आनंदाद्ध्येयवखल्विमानिभूतानिजायंते । आनंदेनजातानिजीवंति । आनंदंप्रयंत्यभिसंविशंतीति ॥ ३ ॥

(Says Varuṇa to Bhrigu)

तपो ब्रह्म इति as meditation and thinking itself is Brahma as Brahma is known by means of it ; स तपः अतप्यत saḥ tapaḥ atapyata, he practised penances ; स तपस्तप्त्वा saḥ tapaḥ taptvâ, and after practising them ; प्राणो ब्रह्म इति व्यजानात् prâṇaḥ brahma iti vyajânât and, was convinced that breath was Brahma ; प्राणात् from breath-god ; हि hi, because ; खलु khalu, verily ; इमानि भूतानि imâni bhûtâni, these beings ; जायन्ते jâyante, are born ; प्राणेन जातानि जीवन्ति prâṇena jâtâni jîvanti, born ones (are able to) live by means of prâṇa ; प्राणं प्रयन्ति अभिसंविशन्ति prâṇam prayanti abhisaṃviśanti, they after death enter prâṇa ; तद्विज्ञाय tadvijñâya after knowing it well ; पुनरेव punaḥ eva, once more ; वरुणं पितरं उपससार varuṇam pitaraṃ upasasâra, went to his father Varuṇa ; saying अधीहि भगवो ब्रह्मेति, oh allow me to study practically Brahma further ; तं हो वाच । तपसा ब्रह्म विजिज्ञासस्व । तपो ब्रह्मेति taṃ ho uvâcha tapasâ brahma vijijñâsasva tapaḥ brahmâ iti, Varuṇa said to Bhrigu, know it by means of constantly practising meditation because meditation is itself Brahma ; स तपो ऽतप्यत । स तपस्तप्त्वा मनोब्रह्मेति व्यजानात् he meditated and afterwards studied that mind-god was Brahma

मनसो ह्येव खलु इमानि भूतानि जायन्ते मनसा जातानि जीवन्ति । मनः प्रयन्ति अभिसंविशन्ति इति । manasaḥ hi eva khalu imâni bhûtâni jâyante manasâ jâtâni jîvanti manaḥ prayanti abhisaṃviśanti iti, because from mind truly these beings are born and when born are able to live by means of it and at the time of death enter the mind-god ; तद्विज्ञाय tatvijñâya, after knowing that Brahma is Mind-god ; पुनरेव वरुणं पितरं उपससार अधीहि भगवो ब्रह्मेति । again Bhrigu went to his father Varuṇa saying ; "Teach me O Lord (more of) Brahma". तं होवाच । तपसा ब्रह्म विजिज्ञासस्व तपो ब्रह्मेति, Him Varuṇa replied "study by means of Tapas, because tapas itself is Brahma"; स तपोऽतप्यत स तपस्तप्त्वा विज्ञानं ब्रह्मेति व्यजानात् । He practised tapas and afterwards understood that understanding was Brahma.

विज्ञानात् हि एव खलु इमानि भूतानि जायन्ते विज्ञानेन जातानि जीवन्ति । विज्ञानं प्रयंति अभिसंविशंति । because from understanding also verily these creatures are born, through it they (are enabled to) live and they enter it ; तद्विज्ञाय, tatvijñâya, after fixing it well in his mind ; पुनरेव वरुणं पितर उपससार । अधीहि ब्रह्म इति, then again he approached Varuṇa his father requesting him to teach Brahma ; तं होवाच to him Varuṇa said ; तपसा ब्रह्म विजिज्ञासस्व । तपो ब्रह्मेति । know it by means of contemplation and practice, because these are themsleves Brahma ; स तपो ऽतप्यत । स तपस्तप्त्वा । आनन्दो ब्रह्मेति व्यजानात् he contemplated and afterwards knew that bliss was Brahma.

आनन्दाद् हि खलु इमानि भूतानि जायन्ते । आनंदेन जातानि जीवन्ति । आनंदं प्रयन्ति अभिसंविशन्ति । Because from bliss these beings are born, by its means they live and in the end they enter it.

3. Penance is Brahma. He performed a penance. He on performing a penance came to know the vital air to be Brahma because from the vital air are born all these created beings by the vital air, the beings live and into the vital air they ultimately merge. Knowing it, he again went to Varuna his father 'Teach me Brahma O! master." He said to him, "enquire Brahma with penance; penace is Brahma." He performed a penance ; after performing a penance he came to know mind to

be Brahma, because from the mind are born all these created beings, by the mind the beings live and into the mind they ultimately merge. Knowing it he again went to Varuṇa his father. "Teach me Brahma ! O! master." He said to him. "know Brahma by means of the penance ; the penance is Brahma." He performed a penance ; he after performing the penance came to know intelligence to be Brahma, because from intelligence are certainly born all the created beings, by intelligence they live and into intelligence they ultimately merge. Knowing this he again went to Varuṇa his father "Teach me Brahma O ! master." He said to him "know Brahma by means of penance, penance is Brahma." He performed a penance and after performing a penance, he came to know happiness to be Brahma, because from happiness certainly are born all these created beings, by happiness they live and into happiness they ultimately merge.

Commentary.

The verse which is numbered as 3 is connected with the preceeding verse. Brahma is intelligence. Bhrigu again performed a penance and came to know vital air, sight, hearing, mind and speech presided over by Pradyumna &c as Brahma.

सैषा भार्गवी वारुणी विद्या । परमेव्योमन्प्रतिष्ठिता
यएवं वेद प्रतितिष्ठति । अन्नवानन्नादोभवति । महान्भवतिप्रज
यापशुभिर्ब्रह्मवर्चसेन । महान्कीर्त्या ॥ ४ ॥

सा एषा sâ eṣâ, that, this, (which shows that food, breath, mind, intellect, and bliss all these are Brahma) ; भार्गवी Bhârgavî, अनुशिष्टा anuśiṣṭà, learnt by Bhirgu ; वारुणी vâruṇî. वरुणेन, उपदिष्टा Updiṣṭâ, taught by varuṇa ; विद्या vidyâ knowledge (of Brahma) ; परमे व्योमन् (व्योम्नि) प्रतिष्ठिता, परमे parame, in the great ; व्योमन् vyoman, (आकाशे व्योम्नि) O ? thou God called sky or about the sky (God called so) ; प्रतिष्ठिता pratiṣṭhità, is fixed ; परमे व्योमन् प्रतिष्ठिता, means is devoted to learn about the great sky like God, as it discusses Brahma, describes his features and as it studies and actually experiences the thing termed Brahma by means of practice and meditation ; तत्परा इति यावत्, ब्रह्म प्रश्नोत्तरात्, ब्रह्म लक्षणात्. ब्रह्मशब्दाभ्यासात्, यः एवं वेद प्रतितिष्ठति। tatparâ iti yâvat, Brahma praśnottarât Brahma lakṣṇât, Brahmaśabdâ abhyâsât, yaḥ evaṃ veda pratitiṣṭhati, he who knows this and experiences this about Brahma becomes free and remains in Brahma ; अन्नवान् annavân अन्नवत्यः he becomes possessed of food (God in it) ; अन्नादः Annâdaḥ, अन्ननामकं हरिं उपजीवति, feeds himself on (the knowledge about) God-food ; भवति bhavati, becomes ; महान् mahân, great ; प्रजया prajayâ, शिष्यप्रजया, by means of getting disciples and children ; पशुभिः paśubhiḥ, by means of cattle ; ब्रह्मवर्च्चसेन Brahmavarchasena, by means of the Vedic lustre (of knowledge) ; महान् mahân, great ; कीर्त्या kîrtyâ, by means of fame. (He becomes famous).

4. This knowledge given to Bhrigu by Varuṇa is permanently fixed in the high sky ; one who knows it becomes permanently fixed, being a possessor of food becomes an eater of food, becomes great with offspring, cattle and Brahmanic glory and reaches greatness with fame.

Commentary

The verse is in praise of the knowledge which is called after both father and son. It is called Bhârgavi, because it was first taught to Brighu and it is called Vâruṇi because it was taught by Varuṇa. The spiritual knowledge qualified as above is permanently fixed in Hari. The fruit that accrues to a devotee who knows this knowledge is that he being protected by Viṣṇu lives uṇder him, becomes great with sons, disciples, cattle ; Brahmanic glory and fame.

अन्नंननिंद्यात्। तद्व्रतं। प्राणोवाअन्नं। शरीरमन्नादं। प्राणेशरीरं प्रतिष्ठितं। शरीरेप्राणःप्रतिष्ठितः। तदेतदन्नमन्ने प्रतिष्ठितं। सयएतदन्न मन्ने प्रतिष्ठितं वेदप्रतितिष्ठति॥ अन्नवानन्नादोभवति॥ महान्भवतिप्रजयापशुभिर्ब्रह्मवर्चसेन महान्कीर्त्या। अन्नंनपरिचक्षीत। तद्व्रतं॥ ५॥

अन्नं annaṃ, अन्नं भगवंतम्, the God food ; न निंद्यात् na nindyât, one should not censure food ; तद् tad, that (the above sentence) ; व्रतम्, vratam, ज्ञातिनः सुखेप्सोः व्रतम् । the rule (of the wise person wishing to be happy) ; प्राणो वा अन्नं prâṇaḥ vâ annaṃ, प्राणो वै अन्नं देहस्थ प्राणागतः प्राणनामाहरिः अन्त नामको वै । the prâṇa god is food ; शरीरं śarîraṃ, body ; शरं जीवं, ईरयति प्रेरयति । तत् जीवप्रेरकं जीवस्थरूपं (भगवत:) शरीरं । that form of God which remains in life and inspires or stimulates the life (for work) ; अन्नादं annâdaṃ, eater of food ; अन्नाख्य रूपानुभवितृ annâkhya rûpânubhavitṛi, that form which experiences the food form of God. Also it can be similarly said ; प्राणो अन्नादः प्राणो शरीरं प्रतिष्ठतम् प्राणाख्ये प्राणाख्यरूपे शरीराख्यं जीवनियंतृरूपं प्रतिष्ठितम् । the Body-God which rules the Jîva is settled in the Breath-God in breath ; शरीरे प्राणः प्रतिष्ठितः शरीराख्ये रूपं प्राणाख्यो हरिः प्रतिष्ठितः । the Prâṇa-God is settled in the Body-God; सः he ; यः who ; एतद् रूपद्वयं this couple of forms ; अन्नं अन्ने प्रतिष्ठितं । being food, each of them exists in the other; वेद veda, knows प्रतितिष्ठति becomes free and then settled ; he becomes, अन्नवान्, अन्नादः, प्रजया, पशुभिः, ब्रह्मवर्च्चसेन...महान् offspring and disciples कीर्त्या (महान्) the meaning of this is already given ; अन्नं न परिचक्षीत, (Parichakṣîta). अन्नाख्यभगवत्परिवर्जनं न कार्यं । one should not abandon food ; तद्व्रतं: tad vratam, that is the rule for a wise man who wishes to get (internal) happiness.

5. Let him not abuse food. It is the vow. Vital air is food ; the body is the eater of food. In the vital air is the body fixed; in the body is the vital air fixed. Therefore this food is fixed in the food. One who knows that this food is fixed in the food becomes permanently fixed, being possessed of food, he becomes an eater of food, becomes great with offspring, cattle and Brahmanic glory and reaches greatness with fame. Let him not abstain from food. It is the vow.

Commentary.

Anna means the Lord. Let him not speak ill of the Lord ; it is the vow of those who are advanced in spiritual science. Hari who pervades the vital air is food. The eater of food is the body pervaded by the soul which stimulates it to act. Both the body and vital air are connected with each other. Hari pervading the vital air is in the body : the body pervaded by the soul is in the vital air. In other words both the enjoyer and the enjoyed are mutually dependent on each other. The fruit that accrues to the devotee who understands the mutual relationship of the enjoyer and the enjoyed is the same as that mentioned in the previous verse. One should not therefore disregard the Lord ; this is the practice (vow) of one who is well versed in the spiritual science,

आपोवान्नं । ज्योतिरन्नादं । अप्सुज्योतिः प्रतिष्ठितं । ज्योतिष्यापः प्रतिष्ठिताः । तदेतदन्नमन्ने प्रतिष्ठितं । सयएतदन्नमन्ने प्रतिष्ठित वेदप्रतितिष्ठति । अन्नवानन्नादोभवति । महान्भवति प्रजयापशुभिर्ब्रह्मवर्चसेन । महान्कीर्त्या । अन्नं बहु कुर्वीत ॥ तद्व्रतं पृथ्वीवाअन्न आकाशोन्नादः । पृथिव्यामाकाशःप्रतिष्ठितः । आकाशेपृथिवीप्रतिष्ठिता । तदेतदन्नमन्नेप्रतिष्ठितं । सयएतदन्नमन्नेप्रतिष्ठितंवेदप्रतितिष्ठति । अन्नवानन्नादोभवति । महान्भवति प्रजयापशुभिर्ब्रह्मवर्चसेन । महान्कीर्त्या ॥ ६ ॥

आपो वै अन्नम् Âpaḥ vâi anannm, अप्सुगतः अप्सुस्थितः अ......हरिः अन्ननामको हरिर्वै । the water God is Food ; ज्योतिः jyotiḥ, light (God); अन्नादम् ânnâdam, that which experiences the form of food ; अप्सु ज्योतिः प्रतिष्ठितम् apsu jyotiḥ pratiṣṭhitam, the Light-God exists in the Water-God ; ज्योतिष्यापः प्रतिष्ठितः, the Water God exists in the Light-God ; तद् that food, एतद्, the couple of forms of light and water existing in each other, food exists in food ; स य एतदन्नं अन्ने प्रतिष्ठितं वेद प्रतिष्ठिति । अन्नवानन्नादो भवति । महान् भवति प्रजया पशुभिः ब्रह्मवर्च्चसेन । महान् कीर्त्या ! he who knows that the Food-God exists in food-God becomes free and settled. He becomes great by getting children and disciples, cattle, and the Brahmic lustre and he becomes very famous ; अन्न बहु कुर्वीत annaṃ bahu kurvît, अन्ने बहुमान बुद्धिः कार्या । बहु गुणकर्मवत्त्वेन अन्ननामकं प्रतिपादयेत् । one should pay great respect to Food (saying that it is great) also he should say that many are the qualifications and actions of food (God); तद्व्रतम् tadvratam, that is the rule for the seeker of Brahma ; पृथिवी वै अन्नं prithivî vai annaṃ, the earth God is the Food-God ; आकाशोऽन्नादः the âkâśa-God experiences the Food-God

(ether) ; पृथिव्यामाकाशः प्रतिष्ठितः prithivyâ mâkâśaḥpratiṣṭaḥ, the ether God rests in the earth-God ; आकाशे पृथिवी प्रतिष्ठिता, the earth-God rests in the ether-God ; तद्, that Food-God ; एतद् this couple of forms (of God) ; रूपद्वयं, the ether and the earth ; these two, because of their resting in each other prove that the food-God is in the food God ; स य एतदन्नमन्ने प्रतिष्ठितं वेद प्रतितिष्ठति । महान् भवति प्रजया पशुभिः ब्रह्मवर्चसेन । महान् कीर्त्या । the meaning is already given.

6. Water is certainly food ; fire is the eater of food ; in waters, is fire permanently fixed ; in the fires is the water fixed. Therefore this food is permanently fixed in the food. One who understands that this food is fixed in the food becomes permanently fixed; being possessed of food, he becomes an eater of food, and great with offspring, cattle and Brahmanic glory and reaches greatness with fame. Let him respect food; it is a vow; the earth is certainly food: the sky is the eater of food. In the earth the sky is permanently fixed ; in the sky the earth is fixed : therefore this food is permanently fixed in the food. One who understands that this food is fixed in the food, becomes permanentaly fixed; being possessed of food becomes an eater of food, and great with offs pring, cattle and Brahman ic glory and reaches greatness with fame.

Commentary.

The verse does not require much elucidation ; the water is described as food and the earth is similarly described. The rest is explained in the comentary on the preceding verse .

नकंचनवसतौप्रत्याचक्षीत। तद्व्रतं । तस्माद्ययाकयाचविधयाबह्वन्नंप्राप्नुयात् । आराध्यस्माअन्नमित्याचक्षते । एतद्वैमुखतोन्नँराद्धं । मुखतोस्माअन्नँराधयते । एतद्वैमध्यतोन्नंराद्धं । मध्यतोस्माअन्नँराध्यते । एतद्वाअंततोन्नँराद्धं अन्ततोस्माअन्नँराध्यते । यएवंवेद ॥ ७ ॥

न कंचन na kaṃchana, none whatsoever (who has come as a student); वसतौ vasatau, निवासस्थाने in his residency; प्रत्याचक्षीत pratyâchakṣita, should he abandon, (he the teacher, the wise man, seeker of Brahma); तद् व्रतम्, that is a rule (for him); तस्माद् tasmâd, ज्ञातस्य अन्नप्रतिष्ठाहेतुत्वात् therefore, because what is learnt (studied) is done through the object of making food great (for the purpose of praying and knowing Food-God); यया कया च विधया yayâ kayâ cha vidhayâ, येन केनापि प्रकारेण any how; बहु अन्नं annam प्राप्नुयात्। अन्नं the food-god; बहु बहुत्वेनमत्वा thinking it to be great and of many forms, qualities and action; प्राप्नुयाद् prâpnuyâd, should attain or get it; अति प्रयत्नेन अपि विहितप्रकारेण बहुतरां भगवद्विपयां प्राप्नुयात्। The sense being that the seeker of Brahma should acquire the knowledge of God in many right or prescribed ways more and more even at the cost of hard labour; अराध्यस्मा अन्नं इति आचक्षते। अस्मै अन्नं आराधि इति आचक्षते। अस्मै asmai, अन्नं बहु इति मन्यमानाय for him who knows that Food-God is manifold; अन्नं the form of God (called अन्नाख्यं भगवद्रूपं) आराधि ârâdhi, सिद्धं भवति is cooked (is ready when taken with God) अस्मै अन्नं आराधि इति आचक्षते they (the wise men विद्वांस:) say; एतत् अन्नं, this food-form of God; वै, surely; मुखतः mukhataḥ, from the very beginning, from the very childhood of the seeker; राद्धं râddhaṃ, तीव्रोपासनयाविज्ञातं चेत्, If known by means of hard worship and practice (by the seeker); मुखतः from the beginning of the food form of God, from his feet; अस्मै उपासकाय for this devotee; अन्नं the food; राध्यते râdhyate, सिध्यति, is ready. The whole means:—a devotee who begins his practice from his very child-hood on the form of God (as a person) is presented from the very beginning of the body the feet, till the end the head; पादावारभ्य शिरः पर्यन्तं सर्वावयवोपेतंरूपं दृश्यते। एतद्वै मध्यतो अन्नं राद्धं if he begins to worship this Food-God in his man-hood (which is the middle of his age); मध्यतोस्मा अन्नं राध्यते। the personal form of the Food-God is presented to him only as the middle portion of the person, the other limbs being so dazzling as to be indistinct to his eyes; एतद्वै अन्ततोऽन्नं राद्धं। if he begins to practise it in his old age; अन्तोतोऽस्मै अन्नं राध्यते। he sees the form of God only from the end. He sees only the feet of the person and the rest of the body as dazzling as light and therefore indistinct. य एवं वेद He who knows this, (secret of the forms) is able to see the whole person of the Food-God.

7. No one should be disregarded (on his arrival) on the house. This is the vow (rule); one should, therefore

procure sufficient food by some means or other. They say 'he supplied him food'. This food is certainly supplied in the beginning; the food is supplied to him in the beginning. The food is certainly supplied in the middle; the food is supplied to him in the middle. The food is verily supplied in the end; the food is supplied to him in the end. One who knows it.

Commentary.

When a student happens to come to the house of a householder his duty is not to refuse him food; he should be given a fit reception; he should procure food for him by some means or other. Such a host who supplies food to a guest is called by the learned men, as a worshipper of the Lord. To one who worships the Lord in the prime of life, He becomes visible to him in full; if one worships him in the middle part of his life only, the middle part but not the whole body of the Lord is visible to him; if one worships him at the last stage of life, he sees the feet only and the rest of the Lord's body appears shining and brilliant like the sun. The same fruit accrnes to him who understands the above said mystery.

क्षेम इति वाचि । योगक्षेम इति प्राणापानयोः कर्म्मेतिहस्तयोः । गतिरितिपादयोः । विमुक्तिरितिपायौ । इति मानुषीः समाज्ञाः । अथदैवीः । तृप्तिरितिवृष्टौ । बलमिति विद्युति । यशइतिपशुषु । ज्योतिरितिनक्षत्रेषु । प्रजातिर मृतमानदइत्युपस्थे । सर्वमित्याकाशे ॥ ८ ॥

क्षेम इति वाचि, वाचि Vâchi वागिन्द्रिये In the organ of speech; क्षेम Kṣema, क्षेम कृतत्वहेतुना क्षेमनामकोहरिः । good-God named Good; one should worship the God-Good in the organ of speech, because it does good; योगक्षेम इति प्राणापानयोः । योग इति प्राणे, क्षेम इति अपाने, as applying in action in the heart and as doer of Gocd in the apâna; कर्म इति हस्तयोः karma iti hastayoḥ, on the hands as action or agent; गतिः इति पादयोः gatiḥ iti pâdayoḥ, as motion or movement in the feet; विमुक्तिः इति पायौ vimuktiḥ iti pâyau; as letting out (the God doing this action) in the anus; इति मानुषीः समाज्ञाः । मानुषी. mânuṣiḥ, pertaining to a human body; समाज्ञाः samâjñâh, उपास्तयः उक्ताः, are told as the actions of worship (or plans of worship in the human body) ; अथ दैवीः atha daivih, now in a Divine body ; तृप्तिः इति वृष्टौ triptih iti vriștau, worship him in the rain as 'Satisfaction" ; बलम् इति विद्युति balam iti vidhyuti, in the electrical sparks as " Force or energy" ; यशः इति पशुषु yaśâh iti paśusu, as " Glory" in the beasts ; ज्योति रिति नक्षत्रेषु Jyotih iti nakșatreșu, as " light " in the stars ; प्रजातिः, अमृतं, आनन्द, इति उपस्थे as " procreation, continuation of the line and bliss" in the reproductive organ; सर्वमिति आकाशे In the space (ether or sky) as "All and everything"; आकाशे, प्रकृतौ ether nature.

8. 'Acquision' in the tongue; acquisition' and 'protection' in the vital air and the filthy air ; 'action', in the hands ; 'loco notion' in the feet ; 'discharge' (of the fœcal matter) in the anus. It is human worship. Now as regards divine ; 'satisfaction' in the rains ; procreation, immortality and happiness in the male organ of generation ; every thing in the sky.

Commertary,

One should worship 'Hari' mentioned here in the text as 'acquisition' fixing the attention in the tougue ; he should worship him as acquisition and protection by fixing his attention on the vital air and the filthy air. In the text the words used are y'ogakșema ' : the yoga means 'acquistion of new things'. 'Kșema' means 'protection of the acquired things'. Similary you have to fix your attention on hands, feet and anus by reason of their performaing manual work, locomotion and evacuation of the bowels. This is the human mode of worship ; now as to the divine mode of worship. Hari by bestowing satisfaction should be worshipped as the rain God ; by bestowing strength, he should be worshipped as lightening in the air, by causing force, he should be worshipped in the animals, as Dakșa Prajâpati and by bestowing offspring, continuation of the family line and family pleasure, he should be worshipped as S'iva. By bestowing favour to all, he is in the ether.

तत्प्रतिष्ठेत्युपासीत । प्रतिष्ठावान्भवति । तन्महइत्युपासीत । महान्भवति । तन्मनइत्युपासीत । मानवान्भवति । तन्नमइत्युपासीत । नम्यंतेस्मैकामाः । तद्ब्रह्मे त्युपासीत । ब्रह्मवान्भवति । तद्ब्रह्मणःपरिमरइत्युपासीत । पर्येणंम्रियंते द्विषंतःसपत्नाः परियेप्रियाभ्रातृव्याः ॥ ६ ॥

तत्, Brahmâ ; प्रतिष्ठा इति, as a support, setting, fixedness ; उपासीत one should worship (the seeker) or (if one worships) ; प्रतिष्ठावान् भवति, (then) he becomes supported, fixed or settled, (i. e, free and immortal by getting salvation) ; मह इति उपासीत, if one worships it as great ; (स) महान्भवति he becomes great ; तन्मन इति उपासीत, if he worships it as respect and mind the organ of knowledge, then (स) मानवान् (mânavân) भवति, he becomes respected ; नम इति, as salutation. नम्यते namyate, नमन्ति आयान्ति, come to, अस्मै उपासकाय, to this worshipper ; कामाः काम्यमाना अर्थाः desired objects ; तद् आकाशे स्थितं ब्रह्म, Brahma in âkâśa; ब्रह्म, पूर्ण ब्रह्म, the perfect Brahma ; ब्रह्मवान् (Brahmavân) भवति possessed of Brahma; become wholly able ; तद् आकाशस्थं ब्रह्म, the Âkâśa Brahmâ ; ब्रह्मणः विरंचेः of Brahmâ ; परिमरः parimaraḥ मारकः, destroyer ; परि pari, परितः, those (द्विषन्तः) round एनं evam, this devotee ; म्रियन्ते mriyante, die ; द्विषन्तः dviṣantaḥ, those who hate ; सपत्नाः sapatnâḥ, enemies, outward ; परियेऽप्रिया भ्रातृव्याः, परि pari, those who are round us ; अप्रिया भ्रातृव्या apriyâ bhrâtrivyâḥ, देहस्थितशत्रवः, the enemies in the body like desire, anger &c., (those who die) ; that no difference should be made between the various forms of God (Viṣṇu) ; he says यश्च अयं पुरुषे, he who is in the body of the person, यश्च असौ आदित्ये, he who is in the sun.

9. Let him worship it as permanence, he becomes permanent ; let him worship it as great, he becomes great ; let him worship it as mind, he becomes respectable ; let him worship it as 'salutation', all desires bow down to him ; let him worship it as Brahma, he becomes full of Brahma. Let him worship it as killer round Brahma, the hostile enemies round him die and those unloving foes also who surround him.

Commentary.

The verse enjoins worship of Brahma as permanent ; by so doing, a worshipper becomes permanent ; by worshipping Brahma as great, the worshipper becomes great ; he becomes respectable by worshipping him as mind ; all his desires are fulfilled, if he worships him in the shape of salutation ; he becomes complete and full, if he worships him as Brahma ; his enemies are destroyed, if a worshipper adores Brahma as killer of all enemies around him : even the enemies in the body such as anger, lust &c, are eradicated entirely on worshipping him.

सयश्चायंपुरुषे । यश्चासावादित्ये । सएकः । सयएवं वित् । अस्माल्लोकात्प्रेत्य । एतमन्नमयमात्मानमुपसंक्रम्य । एतंप्राणमयमात्मानमुपसंक्रम्य । एतंमनोमयमात्मानमुपसंक्रम्य । एतंविज्ञानमयमात्मानमुपसंक्रम्य । एतमानंदमयमात्मानमुपसंक्रम्य । इमाँल्लोकान्कामान्नीकामरूप्यनुसंचरन् । एतत्सामगायन्नास्ते । हा३वुहा३ वुहा३वु । अहमन्नमहमन्नमहमन्नं । अहमन्नादो३हमन्नादो३ हमन्नादः । अहँ श्लोककृदहँ श्लोककृदहँ श्लोककृत् ॥ १० ॥

स एक, this and that is one and the same ; स य एवंवित्, he who knows this. (The above unity of Brahma) ; अस्माद् लोकात् प्रेत्य, after dying ; एतमन्नमयं आत्मानं उपसंक्रम्य etam aunamayaṇ âtmânam upaśaṃkramya, after reaching this food-God ; एतम् mind or (knowledge-God) ; the understanding-God, the Bliss-God ; कामान्नी kâmânnî, कामभोगवान्, enjoing the desired objects ; कामरूपी, kâmarûpî इच्छाधीनरूपवान् taking the desired forms ; इमान् लोकान् अनुसचरन् (anusamcharan), wandering through these worlds ; एतत् सामगायन आस्ते etat sâmagâyan âste, remains singing this Sama Verse. The verse is हा ३ वुहा ३ वुहा ३ वु Oh ! Oh so great ! everywhere ! every wherse अहमन्नं, I am food (object) that can be enjoyed ; अहमन्नादः, I am the food-eater, the agent, the actor there ; अहं श्लोककृत् (ślokakrit) I am the composer of the verses celebrating the greatness and fame

10. He who is in the man and he who is in the sun are one (and the same) ; he who understands it, on departure from this world after becoming the self made of food, after becoming the self made of vital air, after becoming the self made of mind, after becoming the self made of intelligence after becoming the self made of happiness and after roaming over these regions according to his wishes on assuming the desired forms, remains singing the Sâma song "Havu, hâvu hâvu, I am food, I am eater, I am eater, I am a maker of a verse, I am a maker of a verse, I am a maker of a verse"

Commentary.

The opening part of the verse has already been explained in the second Valli, verse 21. He who understands the mystery after assuming all the five bodies mentioned in the text, on death wanders singing Sâma song throughout all the regions, " I am food, I am the eater and I am a singer of the Lord's praise '.

अहमस्मि प्रथमजा ऋता३स्य । पूर्वंदेवेभ्यो मृतस्यना ३ भाइ । योमाददाति स इदेवमा ३ वाः । अहमन्नमन्न मदंतमाद्मि । अहं विश्वं भुवनमभ्यभवां ॥ सुवर्णज्योतीः । य एवंवेद । इत्युपनिषत् ॥ सहनाववतु । सहनौभुनक्तु । सहवीर्यं करवावहै । तेजस्विनावधीतमस्तुमाविद्विषावहै । ओं३ शांतिः शांतिः शांतिः ॥११॥ इति तृतीय वल्ली संम्पूर्णा ।

अहम्, I (Brahma) ; अस्मि, am ; प्रथमजः prathamajaḥ, the first born ; ऋता३स्य Ritâ3sya यद् ऋतं अस्य, from what is called the Right (the God Viṣṇu) ; देवेभ्यः पूर्वं before Gods were born (not mind before men were born) ; मुक्तस्य muktasya, मुक्तवर्गस्य, of the free souls ; ना३भाइ nâ3bhâi nâbhiḥ, the support ; यः he who, an able man of such position ; माः mâḥ प्रभा विष्णुमहिमाप्रतिपादकप्रमाणानि authorities that would prove the greatness of Viṣṇu ; स अधिकारी refers to यः इदेव इत्थमेव in this very way ; मा, मां (to) me ; आवाः आगच्छति comes to me (Brahma) ; अहं अन्नं (हरेः) I am an object of enjoyment to God ; अन्नमदंतं annamadaṇtaṃ, that which enjoys objects, Jîvas. अद्मि admi, I enjoy (all that can enjoy objects) ; अहं, विश्वं whole, all, भुवनं universe ; अभ्यभवं abhyabhavam, श्रेष्ठोस्मि am superior (to the whole of unievrse), (सर्वैं गुणैः) as I possess all the good qualities ; सुवर्णं ज्योतिः, the golden light giver and possessor, God ; य एवं वेद, he who knows this perfectly well. Then the शान्तिः

11. I am the first born of the right or truth. I am the navel of the immortality before the gods ; he who gives me, protects me also . I am food, food, I eat the eating being ; I conquered the worldly regions ; I am like the light of heaven. One who knows this ; this is the mystery.

Om, let him protect us (both) together ; let him nourish us (both) together ; let us (both) show strength, let our learning be splendid ; let us (both) be not hostile (to each other). Om ! peace, peace, peace.

Commentary.

I am the firse born of Hari even before the gods ; I am the centre or support of the salvation. A teacher who advances reason to support the glory of Hari, comes to me here in the state of salvation. Ânanda Tîrtha takes 'avâ, to mean 'to come'. The liberated soul continues saying, "I am food of Hari; all the beings are my food. I have excelled the whole universe by my good qualities ; in other words, I am best of all. I am stimulated to act by Hari who is resplendent like gold". One who understands this mystery obtains the position of a liberated soul singing sàma praises of the Lord. The verse ends with the usual prayer of peace with which it commenced.

End of Bhrigu Valli.

End of Taittirîya Upaniṣad.